The Ramayana

The Ramayana

An Indian Epic

LEKHA WICKRAMASEKARAN

THE RAMAYANA
AN INDIAN EPIC

iUniverse books may be ordered through booksellers or by contacting:

iUniverse
1663 Liberty Drive
Bloomington, IN 47403
www.iuniverse.com
1-800-Authors (1-800-288-4677)

Because of the dynamic nature of the Internet, any web addresses or links contained in this book may have changed since publication and may no longer be valid. The views expressed in this work are solely those of the author and do not necessarily reflect the views of the publisher, and the publisher hereby disclaims any responsibility for them.

Any people depicted in stock imagery provided by Thinkstock are models, and such images are being used for illustrative purposes only. Certain stock imagery © Thinkstock.

ISBN: 978-1-4917-5972-1 (sc)
ISBN: 978-1-4917-5973-8 (hc)
ISBN: 978-1-4917-5971-4 (e)

Library of Congress Control Number: 2015906828

Print information available on the last page.

iUniverse rev. date: 06/29/2015

CONTENTS

To my father, Sittampalam Ariathurai, and to my father-in-law, T.K. Rajasekaran - who were Hindus - and to my mother, Ranjitham Ariathurai, who emphasized the importance of learning the Tamil Language.

Introduction

The great poet Valmiki transcribed this Indian epic, *Ramayana*, more than two thousand years ago. Though the exact date is not known, he was the first to write the story that had been in existence for many generations before him. His writings did not portray Rama as an incarnation of God but as an exceptional man with special powers. It was later translations of this story that portrayed Rama as an incarnation of Lord Vishnu.

Valmiki wrote this poem in twenty-four thousand stanzas in Sanskrit, an ancient Indian language. Indians, of all ages and varied backgrounds, know the essential part of the story. An eleventh-century poet named Kamban wrote the best-known Tamil translation of this epic. This is an abridged version to let the readers know the teachings as Kamban understood *The Ramayana*. Descriptions in the original version are more eloquent and have been condensed or altogether left out. Most of the stories related in the original have been translated.

Tamil is the oldest living language—a Dravidian language still spoken by millions in different parts of the world. Kamban translated *Ramayana* from the original work written in Sanskrit but composed the poem again in his own poetry—10,500 stanzas written in Tamil and stamped on palm leaves.

The Ramayana is not history or biography but part of Hindu sacred narrative, just as Greek and Roman mythologies are to the Greek and Roman civilizations, respectively. Mythology, philosophy, and rituals are the three cornerstones of all ancient religions. Hinduism is no different. Tradition and holy figures provide guides and inspiration that serve as a foundation for any great culture, as do Rama, Sitha, Lakshmana, Bharatha, and Hanuman.

The Ramayana, a well-written epic with impressive characters that have been admired and withstood the passage of time, is a literary masterpiece that lends itself to deep discussions and character analysis, as it is the age-old story of good fighting evil. It is a scripture in Hinduism.

As we get more familiar with *The Ramayana*, the epic teaches us lessons applicable for all time and all conditions of life. Loyalty, heroism, courage, and strong family ties are characteristics common to the good and the bad alike.

Children in India are familiar with this story, as it has been told to them sometime in their lives. Indians have travelled everywhere and settled in different parts of the globe. Unlike in foreign lands, family units in India most often include three generations of close-knit family members. There usually is someone who has the time and inclination to relate *The Ramayana* to the younger generation. Abroad, as opposed to in

India, *The Ramayana* is not a general play enacted in a hall or the village green, or studied as a scripture or literature, or taught in schools and temples.

The following pages, based mostly on Kamban's translation, are an attempt to tell the story of Rama and Sitha to those, young and old, unfamiliar with this great epic. It is an effort to bridge the gap that is developing, by passing down this story to the coming generations. This translation is directed to readers who are unfamiliar with life in India and the similarities in culture then and now. Unlike other narratives of this epic, the author attempts to relate the story as told by Kamban and does not insert her opinion or standards.

The Indian people used this legend as a vehicle to give insight into the social code, religion, and ethics. Customs and rituals revealed in this tale have been followed generation after generation, and familiarity with them enables a better understanding of the Indian people and their culture.

Prologue

All the gods appealed to the Supreme God, Vishnu, for his help. They said, "Ravana, the ten-headed king of the Rakshasas, and his brothers acquired extraordinary powers from us through self-denial and prayers. Now, using these powers, they practice tyranny and evil, suppressing all virtue and goodness wherever they find it. They threaten to destroy our worlds and make us slaves. Shiva, the Destroyer, is unable to support. Brahma, the Creator, can do very little. These two gods originally granted Ravana and his brothers these powers, and as such, they cannot withdraw it. You are the Protector and the greatest of the gods and should save us."

MahaVishnu promised, "Ravana can be killed only by a human or animals since he never asked for protection from them. I shall incarnate as Dasaratha's sons ..."

The joyous gods created a race of giant monkeys whose courage, strength, and wisdom would help Vishnu (incarnated as all four sons of Dasaratha) destroy Ravana, the king of the Rakshasas, and those who helped him.

List of Characters

Main Characters

Dasaratha: King of Kosala country with Ayodhya as its capital. He had three wives and four sons.

Rama: The hero of this story; son of King Dasaratha and Queen Kausalya; believed to be the first incarnation of Vishnu.

Bharatha: A noble and honorable son of King Dasaratha and Queen Kaikeyi and the second incarnation of Vishnu.

Lakshmana: Son of King Dasaratha and Queen Sumithra, very loyal to Rama, and the third incarnation of Vishnu.

Sathrugna: Son of King Dasaratha and Queen Sumithra and the fourth incarnation of Vishnu and Lakshmana's twin.

Kausalaya: First wife of Dasaratha and mother of Rama.

Kaikeyi: Favorite wife of Dasaratha and mother of Bharatha.

Sumithra: Wife of Dasaratha and mother of twins, Lakshmana and Sathrugna.

Viswamithra: Sage and teacher to the young Rama. He knew that Rama was an incarnation of Vishnu.

Kooni: Kaikeyi's evil maid who bore a grudge against Rama.

Sumanthra: Chief minister and charioteer to King Dasaratha.

Visishtha: Royal priest to King Dasaratha.

Guha: Chieftain of the tribes who live on the banks of the Ganges.

King Janaka: King of Videha country with Mithila as its capital.

Sitha: Wife of Vishnu, Goddess Lakshmi, and Janaki, and daughter of Mother Earth. Incarnate as a foundling, adopted by King Janaka and his wife. She is the heroine of *The Ramayana* epic.

Lava and Kusa: Rama and Sitha's twin sons.

Characters Rama Encounters on his Journeys

Suketha: Mother of Thataka; a demigod of valor, might, and purity.

Thataka: A demigod turned into a demon (Rakshasa); wife of Sunda.

Sunda: Husband of Thataka; a chieftain.

Agasthya: A sage who lived in the forest that was being destroyed by Sunda and his sons.

Mahabali: A very powerful demon whose evil deeds resulted in Lord Vishnu incarnating as a pigmy to reconquer the worlds he had terrorized.

Vamana: A pigmy who tricked Mahabali and conquered the worlds.

Gautama: A sage/rishi, who cursed his wife, Ahalya, into a stone statue because of infidelity.

Ahalya: Sage Gautama's wife, who was turned into stone and then was later freed from the curse by the touch of Rama.

Bhagiratha: In order to obtain salvation for his ancestors by washing their bones in its waters, he brought the Ganges down to earth. His name is a byword for "indefatigable effort."

The Rakshasas

Ravana: Ten-headed king of Lanka, also known as Dashanan.

Vibishana: Ravana's brother who joins Rama and later becomes king of Lanka.

Kumbakarna: Ravana's giant brother, known for sleeping and eating in abundance, was the greatest Rakshasa warrior.

Soorpanaka: A demon, sister to Ravana.

Kara: Ravana's brother.

Dooshana: Ravana's brother.

Mandodari: Ravana's wife.

Indrajit: Ravana's son.

Mayavi: The Rakshasa who challenged Vali to a fight.

*Animal Characters (Gods that Come Down
to Earth as Animals to Help Vishnu)*

Vali: Ruler of a giant monkey race in Kiskinda.

Sugreeva: Vali's brother, who kills him with Rama's help.

Tara: Vali's wife, previously Sugreeva's wife.

Angada: Vali and Tara's son.

Hanuman: The son of the god of wind, Sugreeva's ally, and the greatest devotee of Rama. A great monkey hero, also known as Anjaneya. Many temples have been built in recognition of his greatness.

Jambavan: A wise elder, one of Hanuman's search party, in the form of a bear. The king of the Bears.

Jatayu: King Dasaratha's friend and ally; a god in the form of an eagle.

Sampathi: Jatayu's elder brother, an eagle.

Garuda: The divine eagle that carried Lord Vishnu on his travels.

Hindu Gods

Mahavishnu: The one god who divides himself into the trinity.

Brahma: Four-faced god who is Vishnu in the form of Creator of life on earth.

Vishnu: God without beginning, middle, or end; Vishnu as the protector of the universe and the preserver of life on earth.

Shiva: Vishnu as the destroyer of life on earth.

Indra: Chief of the gods.

Mother Earth: Mother of Sitha.

Lakshmi: Goddess of beauty and good fortune and wife of Vishnu, who incarnated as Sitha.

Agni: God of fire.

Yama: God of death.

Soorya: Son god.

Kubera: God of Wealth.

Vahyna: God of wind and father of Hanuman.

Manmatha: God of love.

Adishesha: God of serpents. The couch that Lord Vishnu used. He incarnated as Lakshmana when Rama came down to earth.

Valmiki: Great Sanskrit poet of the epic *Ramayana*. Sage who helped Sitha and her two sons and let them live in his ashram with his wife.

Figure 1: Royal family tree.

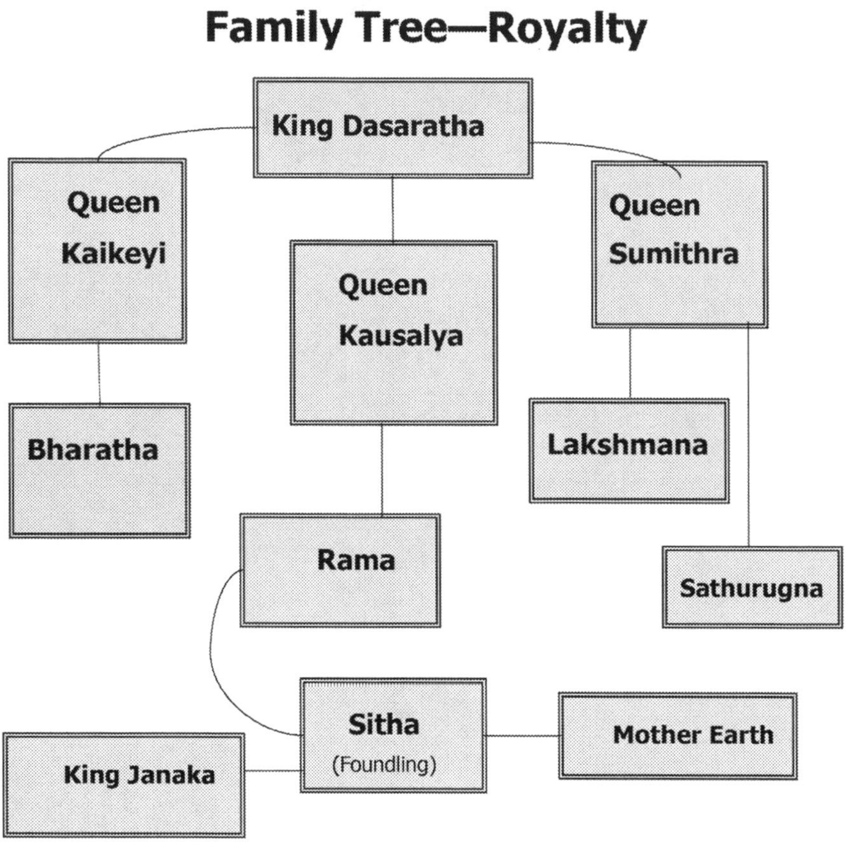

Family Tree—Royalty

Figure 2: The Rakshasas royalty.

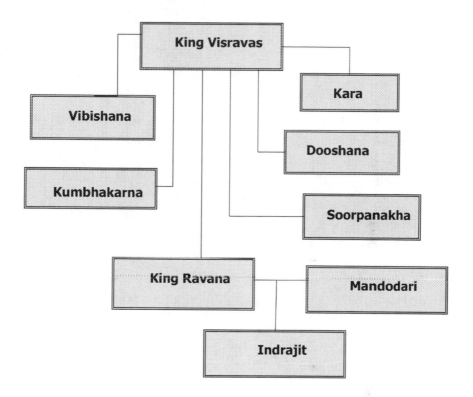

Book 1

Rama

The Young Years

The Birth of Rama

In the ancient land of Bharat, the kingdom of Kosala lay north of the Ganges (Ganga), with the river Sarayu, a tributary of Ganga, running through it. In this mountainous region, white, fleecy clouds drifted toward the sea, returning heavy with water. They approached the mountains, where the clouds then scattered over the Himalayas. On seeing the bountiful riches on the slopes, the clouds condensed as raindrops and formed streams, bringing down the treasures of minerals and essences and merging into a river. Treasures included precious stones brought in from the earth: pollen and peacock feathers carried by the wind; tusks discarded by elephants that came for water; fragrances absorbed in the water from women as they played and swam—petals from flower garlands in their hair, and sandalwood as it washed off their bodies.

On a lazy afternoon, streams meandered down, bubbling and tripping over rocks in their paths, with the sun creating rainbows suspended over them. They met and merged, collected in a crescendo, finally climaxing into a churning, thundering river, threatening to fight the sea. This river Sarayu flowed through mountains and valleys, forests and plains. It broke into smaller tributaries that ran merrily along as it entered into Kosala, making the country fertile and rich. It brought fragrances from nutmeg to sandalwood, which emanated from the water along with various herbs, fruits, and barks from trees. Sometimes it even carried along garments left by women on the banks as they bathed in the streams.

The countryside had many groves and gardens. Lotus blooms floated in the ponds. Inside the groves, lovers met in the arbors, and cuckoo birds sang tunefully. Peacocks spread their colorful tails and danced gracefully.

Outside on the sunlit slopes, men and women were busy with their activities: plowing fields and tilling the soil using bulls; harvesting crops; threshing and separating grains from the chaff; even watching cockfights, cheering and shouting over the squawking birds.

Ayodhya was the capital of Kosala—a city with many mansions, fountains, squares, and white turrets in the skyline. Golden palaces glistened in the sun, and young women walked and talked on the palace balconies. Moats, which were home to many crocodiles, surrounded the palaces. Occasionally the crocodiles fought stubbornly with each other, noisily snapping their jaws. Flat walls covered in silver bordered the orchards surrounding the moat. The parapet wall, built of rows of stones gilded with gold, rose from the moat. Arched entryways, ornately built, faced all eight directions—north, northeast, northwest, east, south, southeast, southwest, and west.

King Dasaratha was compassionate, courageous, and just. He ruled from his grand palace in Ayodhya and was well loved and honored by his subjects. The people of Kosala were happy, virtuous, and content. The citizens wanted for nothing and had plenty, and nobody stole. Taxes were light, and punishment of crime was just. King Dasaratha's greatest sorrow was that he did not have any children. He feared the Solar Dynasty would end with him.

Some time ago, the gods complained to Lord Shiva about the evil that Ravana and his Rakshasas were committing against the gods and humans. Lord Shiva said, "I cannot destroy him. I have granted boons to protect him from such acts. Why don't you ask Lord Brahma to help you?"

The gods went forth to Lord Brahma's abode on the mountain and told him about the problems the Rakshasas caused.

Immediately Brahma said, "Once in his travels, Ravana went with his followers to the heavens and started fighting with the gods. Ravana won his son Indra in the war, bound him with ropes, carried him to Lanka, and imprisoned him. When I heard this, I intervened and granted him a wish; he would be called Indrajit and brought back Lord Indra. Now I cannot do anything more. It is only if Lord Vishnu feels compassion for you and destroys the Rakshasas that you will live in peace."

Hearing this, the gods thought of Lord Vishnu and gave praise to him in their hearts. Brahma too joined them in silent prayer. Lord Vishnu, hearing their prayers, arrived before them on his faithful, divine eagle, Garuda, accompanied by his wife, Lakshmi. The gods were joyous and fell to their knees in worship. He climbed down from Garuda's shoulders and sat on the seat in the hall. The gods were confident Lord Vishnu would help them when he appeared before them. They recounted to Lord Vishnu the evils the Rakshasas had done.

They said, "The good deeds that are done by those in the heavens and those on earth are destroyed by the Rakshasas. If this goes on, we cannot survive."

Lord Vishnu, seeing their despair, said, "Dear lords, do not worry! I will appear as a human on earth and will vanquish the terrible Ravana and end your sorrows. You must listen to me. You will go down as monkeys and be born in groups in the jungles, the orchards, and the mountains. The conch shell and the wheel that I hold in each hand, and the couch that I always use will incarnate as my brothers and be born to King Dasaratha. I will then fight the Rakshasas and destroy them."

The gods were happy and watched as Lord Vishnu climbed on Garuda's shoulders and disappeared.

Lord Brahma addressed the gods and said, "The mightiest bear, Jambavan, intends to join Lord Vishnu on earth and help him. Be at peace. Go and follow the instructions given you by Lord Vishnu."

One day, King Dasaratha consulted his religious masters. Sage Vasishtha recollected the meeting between the gods to discuss the problems caused by Ravana, but he kept it to himself. He thought that if King Dasaratha's performed a *yagna,* it would allow Lord Vishnu to incarnate as his son and help the gods destroy the Rakshasas.

A yagna was a sacrifice for progeny—a grand affair with royal invitees that went on for a year. The event followed strict rules. Tens of thousands of people attended, and the invitees included princes and sages of the land. A lavish tent-city accommodated the guests, and the host provided lavish hospitality, including food, lodging, and entertainment.

Sage Vasishtha said, "My lord, if you perform a yagna, your sorrow will disappear, and you will have a son."

King Dasaratha followed the sage's advice. At the end of the year, the actual ceremony was performed. At the ceremony, a majestic figure rose from the sacrificial fire with a bowl of rice pudding, *payasam,* sent by the gods for the king's wives, in his palms. King Dasaratha accepted the gift.

He divided the bowl of rice pudding and gave his wives, Kausalya, Kaikeyi, and Sumithra, equal portions. A crow swooped down and went off with Sumithra's payasam. Queens Kausalya and Kaikeyi shared their portions with Queen Sumithra, resulting in Queen Sumithra getting two portions. The queens ate the portions and soon conceived.

After the appropriate period, four baby boys were born. Sage Vasishtha helped name the babies. Kausalya gave birth to Rama; Kaikeyi had Bharatha; and Sumithra had twins, Lakshmana and Sathurugna, in that order.

Sage Vasishtha lived on the outskirts of the palace and taught the boys yoga and philosophy as they grew up. They also learned archery and riding horses, elephants and chariots. The brothers played and studied together and were very happy. Though the brothers were close, Rama had never been apart from Lakshmana, and Bharatha and Sathurugna were inseparable. Everyone loved the princes, especially Rama, who always had a kind word for the citizens whenever he saw them.

Many years later when the boys were still children, Sage Viswamithra visited King Dasaratha and wanted a favor from the king.

"I wish to perform a sacrifice on the other side of the Ganges but need help to overcome the evil creatures that wait to disturb every holy undertaking. The Rakshasas have disrupted us, and we want you to stop them. Could you help me?"

"Of course I will help in any way I can," said the king.

"I just need your son, Prince Rama, to come with me. That would be adequate," the sage replied.

King Dasaratha was very willing to help but was dismayed to find out that the sage wanted only Rama's help.

King Dasaratha refused him, saying, "Not my son Rama. Anyone else, even an army, but not Rama!"

Sage Viswamithra got angry.

Seeing this, Sage Vasishtha stepped in and advised the king, saying, "Accompanying the sage would be the best thing for Rama. Send Lakshmana, too. Your sons will benefit vastly by this. Do not prevent them. Let them go."

The king could not refuse Vasishtha and reluctantly agreed.

King Dasaratha sent for Rama and asked Sage Viswamithra, "Can Lakshmana accompany Rama? They are so young and have never been apart."

The sage agreed. The teenage princes came in and received the blessings of the queens, Vasishtha, and the king.

The king handed them over to the Sage's care, saying, "You will be their mother and their father. Please take good care of them."

Rama and Lakshmana followed the sage to the river Sarayu.

Thataka's Story

Viswamithra and his two young disciples traveled through the green country along the Sarayu River, hearing sounds of the river and animals. Resting at night and walking during the day, they finally reached the Ganges and crossed the river in a raft. In midstream, the boys were startled by a deafening sound. When Viswamithra informed them that the sound was caused by the Sarayu crashing into the Ganges River, the boys were filled with wonder at the two big, holy rivers meeting and becoming one, and silently they said a prayer.

Soon they went through land that was scorched - dry and hot. The sage taught them mantras, and when the boys meditated on these and recited them, they did not feel the heat.

Rama asked, "Why is this land so terrible? Has it been cursed?"

Viswamithra replied, "This is the Dandaka Forest. At one time, it was fertile, beautiful, and well populated. I will tell you the story of Thataka, a woman of great courage and goodness. She was the beautiful daughter of Suketha and was married to Sunda. They had two strong sons who had enormous supernatural powers in addition to physical strength. The sons grew up to be wild and destructive. Their father delighted at their pranks and joined them in destroying ancient trees and killing animals.

"Agasthya was a saint who had his hermitage in the forest. When he saw the destruction caused by Sunda and his unruly sons, he cursed the person responsible, and Sunda fell dead. When Suketha learned of her husband's death, she and her sons stormed into the forest, wanting to avenge Sunda's death. The saint met their challenge by cursing them to demon hood - until now they had been demigods—to live in hell. The three immediately underwent an alteration, becoming threatening in features and stature, as befitting demons.

"The two sons went away looking for super demons - demons having more supernatural power than they had - while the mother stayed behind scorching everything with her fiery breath and turning the beautiful and fertile land into sand and desert. The name of the terrifying creature was Thataka, and she was a threat to the hermits."

Rama said, "Where is she to be found?"

Even as he spoke, the ground shook, and Thataka arrived, her eyes spitting fire, and her lips parted, revealing a cavernous mouth with sharp, oversized fangs.

She rolled her eyes and roared, "Why have you come here? Do you have a death wish? I have crushed and eaten anything that moves in my kingdom, and I welcome you as my next meal!"

She pointed a trident at Rama's chest and said, "I will split your chest right here!" She provided a fearsome spectacle as she loudly ground her teeth.

Rama stood by patiently and silently, and even when she pointed her trident at his chest, he did not flinch. Even with all this provocation, the young prince could not forget that killing a woman, however evil, was a cardinal sin.

Viswamithra said, "Rama! This woman has performed as much evil as is possible. We lost weight because we could not meditate and are mostly skin and bones, and that is why she did not eat us. A woman so evil loses consideration as a woman. It is your duty to rid this world of her. She is a menace!"

Rama capitulated and said, "I will carry out your wish."

Thataka threw her three-pronged spear at Rama. It came, flaming, toward him. Rama strung his bow and released an arrow that hit the spear and broke it into pieces. Next, Thataka sent a hail of stones, but Rama and Lakshmana protected themselves with their arrows. Finally, Rama's arrow pierced Thataka's throat and killed her. With Thataka's death, the spell broke, and the forest transformed and became beautiful. Vegetation grew back, and the flowers and fruits were in abundance. Birds—chirping and singing melodiously—and animals returned. Good had won over evil.

Twilight fell, and Sage Viswamithra, Rama, and Lakshmana spent the night there. Viswamithra, a former warrior and conqueror and a master of weapons, taught Rama all the techniques in weaponry, and Rama grew in knowledge and power. Rama, in turn, taught his brother, Lakshmana. Thus, Rama began his life's mission of destroying evil in this world.

Mahabali's Story

The next morning as Sage Viswamithra, Rama, and Lakshmana continued on their journey, they reached a mountain covered with mist, and Sage Viswamithra told them another story.

"This is hallowed ground where Lord Vishnu once sat in meditation. It was here while Vishnu meditated that Mahabali, a very powerful demon, conquered many kingdoms. The gods who had suffered at Mahabali's hand begged Vishnu to help them regain their kingdoms. Mahabali invited many of the learned men of the land to a sacrifice to celebrate his victories.

"In order to help the gods, Vishnu came down to earth; he entered into a Brahmin family as a person of small stature. When he presented himself at the palace gates, Mahabali's guru warned him that the dwarfish student was actually a god in disguise who had come to earth to destroy him. Disregarding the warning, Mahabali met him and welcomed him warmly.

"The visitor said, 'I have come from a long distance to meet someone of your courage and greatness. Your successes are world-renowned. Now, after meeting you, I am so happy that I have achieved one of my dearest goals!'

"'Do not praise me, O great one!' Mahabali replied. 'I am a warrior and conqueror—base qualities when compared to the learning and achievements of one like you. Appearances can be deceptive. You are great, and I shall be deeply honored if you would accept a gift in return for the esteem you have paid me by your visit.'

"'The honor is mine. I want only your goodwill toward me; that is gift enough. I will take leave of you now.'

"'No—please don't go! Ask for something. Anything! It will give me great pleasure to grant it.'

"'Well … if you insist, then grant me a piece of land.'

"'Yes! You can choose it wherever you wish—however large.'

"'Just what would be measured in three strides of my feet …'

"Mahabali, looking his diminutive figure up and down, laughed and said, 'Is that all?'

"'Yes.'

"Mahabali's guru tried to warn him, 'King, don't let his size deceive you! He is deceiving you!'

"'Is that so? Don't prevent me from giving! If the greatest of all, Vishnu, has come regardless of his high status, I have to give him what he asked for! It would be my honor! Don't stop me!'

"Saying this, Mahabali attempted to pour a little water into the upturned palm of the dwarf to seal the deal.

"The guru made himself into a little bug and settled on the lip of the water vessel to prevent the water from flowing into the dwarf's palm. Seeing this, Vishnu took a blade of grass and poked at the vessel, hurting the bug in one eye! The bug flew away in pain.

"Mahabali poured the water into the upturned palms and said, 'Measure and receive your three steps of earth.'

"The moment the water fell on his hand, the small person became a giant reaching the sky. With the first step, he spanned the entire earth, and the second step covered the heavens. He had acquired the whole universe.

"He asked Mahabali, 'Lord, show me where to place the third step?'

"Mahabali, overawed, kneeling and bowing before him, said, 'Here, on my head, if no other space is available.'

"Vishnu raised his foot, placed it on his head, and pressed him down to the underworld.

"'You are banished and will not torment the world anymore,' he said, and he removed Mahabali so that he and the gods would be left in peace.

"Vishnu went back and returned to his meditation.

"Appearances are often deceptive ..."

Ganga's Story

After traveling for a day, Viswamithra, Rama, and Lakshmana arrived at a valley where the Ganges flowed.

Viswamithra said, "Here you see the holiest river in the world, the river Ganges, starting from the Himalayas and running through the mountains and valleys of many kingdoms. Let me tell you her story."

"In the beginning, earth, one of the five primeval elements— earth, water, fire, air, and ether—was created. Mother Earth has witnessed both good and evil—animals and plants, nature and humans making changes for better or for worse and leaving their imprint long after they are gone. Mother Earth will be there until the end of time. When we probe and understand the history of the ground we traverse daily, we begin to know Mother Earth and appreciate her power and beauty.

"The Ganges starts from the Himalayas, gathers rare herbs and minerals, and flows down to the valley. Every inch of the ground the Ganges touches and cleanses becomes holy: the kingdoms she traverses through become fertile and prosperous; sages meditate by the river; the sick and dying drink the water, not to be healed but to attain salvation—the same reason ashes of the dead are sprinkled in the holy river. Nevertheless, Ganga had to be tamed before she could touch this earth and be as serene and calm as she is now—the river Ganges.

"The king of the mountains and his wife had two daughters. Ganga was the elder daughter, and at the request of the gods, the king sent her to live in heaven with the gods. The younger daughter, Uma, was favored by Lord Shiva and became his wife.

"Sakara, one of your ancestors and a king of Ayodhya, was a good king. He had two wives but no sons. The king made many sacrifices and was rewarded with the birth of numerous sons. One wife had one son while the other gave birth to a mass that divided into sixty thousand baby boys. The sixty thousand boys grew up to be strong, handsome princes while the only son turned out to be a cruel lunatic. People hated him and banished him from the country. Later, he had a son, Amsuman, who was brave and generous; this was the king's grandson.

"King Sakara performed a Horse Sacrifice, with Prince Amsuman in charge. In this kind of sacrifice, a decorated horse was set free to wander at will. The country through which the horse traveled on his journey accepted the owner of the horse as its ruler to control its international affairs. If anyone attempted to hold up the horse, the horse's owner attacked the country where the horse was a captive and set the horse free again. This repeated until the horse returned home.

"The humans who embarked on such a plan could eventually extend their empire and challenge the gods' own superiority!

Finally, Indra, the king of the gods himself, felt threatened. He and the other gods were nervous and watchful whenever there was a Horse Sacrifice planned, and they tried to defeat it.

"For this reason, when Sakara's horse was released for the start of the Horse Sacrifice, Lord Indra abducted the animal and kept it hidden in the deepest underground world. It was a secluded spot behind where Sage Kapila was meditating.

"When the horse was lost in the underground world, King Sakara's sixty thousand sons scoured the earth and started digging wide and deep into the bowels of the earth. Finally they found the horse, tethered behind Sage Kapila as he sat meditating. After capturing their horse and assuming the sage had stolen the horse, they tormented the sage. The sage, disturbed from his prayers, reduced them to ashes with a withering look!

"After the king waited in vain for his sons' return, he sent his grandson, Amsuman, in search of them. Amsuman found the horse grazing contentedly behind Sage Kapila. Amsuman apologized for his uncles' behavior, recaptured the horse, and went looking for all his uncles. In his search, he met Garuda, the bird king.

"Garuda pointed at a heap of ashes lying on the ground and said, 'That is all that is left of your uncles—the sixty thousand sons of Sakura! Go complete the Horse Sacrifice. If Ganga is brought down to earth and touches the remains of your uncles, their souls will be able to rest in peace.'

"Amsuman took the horse and went home to help the old king complete his Horse Sacrifice.

"Eventually, Amsuman inherited the kingdom of Ayodhya from King Sakara. Though Sakara and Amsuman tried to bring Ganga from the heavens down to earth, they never could and died disconsolate at being unable to do so. Eventually, Amsuman's son, Bhagiratha, became king of Ayodhya.

"Bhagiratha grew up determined to help his ancestors attain salvation. He knew that without proper disposal of their remains, they would remain in purgatory. He prayed for ten thousand years to Brahma, the creator, to help him make amends for his ancestors' sins so that their souls could go to heaven. Brahma advised him to seek Lord Shiva's help to bring down Ganga from the high heavens so that he could soak their ashes in its holy waters and cleanse them of their sins.

"He then prayed to Shiva for ten thousand years. Shiva promised to grant him his wish if he could persuade Ganga to descend from heaven. He then prayed to Ganga for five thousand years.

"Ganga appeared disguised as an elegant little girl and said, 'If Ganga, from the heavens, falls directly on earth, it will not be able to bear the weight and speed with which it will crash down. Not only that, only Shiva is capable of supporting Ganga's full force. Shiva promised to help. Find out what Shiva's intentions are. Pray to him again.'

"Saying this, the little girl disappeared.

"After further meditations for eleven thousand years by Bhagiratha, Shiva appeared and said to him, 'Let Ganga come down to earth. I will see that not a drop of water is allowed to fall directly on earth. Don't worry; I will protect the earth.'

"Bhagiratha felt tossed about, but, undaunted and undergoing hardships, he persevered. He prayed for thirty thousand years more.

"At the end of Bhagiratha's penance, Ganga started her roaring deluge and descended from the world of Brahma, the creator. Shiva appeared as promised and planted his feet firmly, arms akimbo, and received the impact of the deluge on his head. The roaring flood thundered down and vanished into his matted locks of hair. Bhagiratha began to feel uneasy at the tame and quiet end of Ganga. All his prayers and penance had produced nothing in the end! He could not dispose of his ancestors' remains if Ganga was not down on earth.

"Shiva understood Bhagiratha's predicament and said, 'Oh faithful one! Don't despair. Ganga from the heavens is now nestled in my hair.'

"Saying this, he let a trickle of water flow out of his locks—and Ganga came down to earth and became the river Ganges! Bhagiratha carefully led it over his ancestors' ashes and helped their souls find salvation. Bhagiratha then returned to his beautiful kingdom of Ayodhya.

"Thus, Bhagiratha's perseverance helped all humanity. The Ganges bears a number of shrines on its banks and nourishes millions of acres of land and people along its course. The pit dug by Sakara's sons while searching for their horse during the Horse Sacrifice filled up and became the oceans of today."

To this day, many believe that those who bathe in the holy waters of the Ganges will be cleansed of sin and endowed with virtue and strength. Many Hindus still sprinkle the ashes of their dead in the divine Ganga for absolution and redemption of their souls.

After listening to the story about the origin of the Ganges River, Rama and Lakshmana were in wonder and prayed to the river. Then the three of them proceeded on toward Mithila.

Ahalya's Story

As night fell, they camped outside the walls of Mithila. They saw the stone statue that was Ahalya. As Rama's feet accidentally brushed against the vertical slab of stone, Ahalya's spell was broken, and she appeared in her human form as a beautiful woman. The woman waited respectfully, and Viswamithra introduced her to Rama.

Viswamithra said to Rama, "O great one with the body the color of a dark cloud, you are born to restore morality and goodness to mankind and eliminate all evil! I saw the power of your arms, and now I see the power of your feet."

Rama said, "O great sage! She appears blameless and pure. If she was turned into stone, what is the state of this world? Is she paying for sins from her past life? Please tell me why she was punished thus."

"This is the wife of Sage Gautama. He is the sage whose curse resulted in Indra's body being studded all over with a thousand eyes." He then told the brothers her story.

"Brahma created an absolutely beautiful woman and called her Ahalya. On seeing her, Lord Indra, the highest god, attracted by her beauty, was sure that he alone was worthy of her. Brahma, disliking Indra's conceit, ignored him and left the girl with Sage Gautama as guardian. Under his care, she grew up into a beautiful young woman.

"When she was old enough, the sage handed her back to Brahma. Brahma appreciated Gautama's purity in thought, word, and deed in the way he had treated his ward, Ahalya. Indra asked for Ahalya's hand in marriage from Brahma, but Brahma did not approve of Indra's conceit and did not favor this union.

"He told Sage Gautama, 'Marry her and take care of her. She is fit to be your wife, and you alone are fit to be her husband.'

"They were married. Ahalya was a perfect wife, and they lived happily.

"Indra was angry and jealous; he had never gotten over his infatuation for Ahalya. He came in many disguises to Gautama's hermitage to lust after Ahalya. He observed the sage's routine, noticing that he left for a couple hours every morning to go to the river for his bath and prayers.

"Overcome by his love for Ahalya, Indra decided to seduce Ahalya. He planned to deceive her after her husband left in the morning. Unable to contain himself any longer, he crowed like a rooster and tricked the sage into thinking it was morning. Indra's impatience resulted in the sage leaving for the river earlier than usual.

"Indra then assumed the sage's form, entered the hut, and started making love to Ahalya. She surrendered herself but realized from the scent emanating from Indra that this was not her husband. She realized it was Indra, and, forgetting it would hurt her virtue, she did nothing to stop him.

"Gautama realized something was wrong; it was too early in the morning. He went back to his home and surprised the couple making love.

"Ahalya, ashamed and remorseful, tearfully said, 'We have been deceived by Indra!'

"Indra assumed the form of a cat and tried to slip away. The sage was not deceived.

"He said, 'Cat, I know your obsession with one woman's vagina has caused you to sin by coveting another man's wife. So that you will not be tempted, may your body be covered with a thousand vaginas! People in all the worlds may realize what goes on in your mind at all times!'

"A thousand vaginas covered Indra's body. There could be no greater shame for the vain Indra. Ashamed, he left for his world.

"After Indra left, Gautama looked at his wife and said, 'Ahalya, beauty is a virtue for women. You strayed and behaved like a whore. You have sinned with your body. May that body harden into a shapeless piece of granite where you stand!'

"Ahalya was slowly turning to stone.

"In desperation, she begged, 'My lord! Please forgive me for this sin that I committed without my knowledge. A grave mistake has been committed. Is there no end to this curse? Please ... I feel a weight creeping up my feet. Do something ...'

"The sage felt sorry for her and granted an end to the curse, saying, 'Woman, your redemption will come when the son of Dasaratha, Rama, passes this way at some future date and his footstep touches you …'

"The errant wife, Ahalya, became a stone statue.

"Meanwhile, Indra was embarrassed and ashamed of his appearance. He kept to himself and hid in darkness, not going out even to perform his duties. He became poverty stricken, and the other gods suffered. This concerned the gods, as his tasks in various worlds remained undone. They went to Brahma to ask him to intercede with Gautama.

"By this time, the sage's anger had subsided, and he said, 'May the thousand additions to Indra's body become eyes.'

"Indra was thereafter known as the 'thousand-eyed god.' The gods, including Indra, went back to their various worlds and continued to perform their duties."

Rama said to Ahalya, "Mother, go in peace! Do not grieve over what is past and gone, thus preventing you from finding the happiness you deserve. May you find your revered husband, live in his service, and earn his compassion and affection again."

Saying this, the travelers continued on with their journey, leaving Ahalya. Approaching Mithila, they stopped to rest at Gautama's hermitage. Gautama had been praying at the foot of the Himalayas for the sins caused by cursing Ahalya and Indra.

Viswamithra told Sage Gautama, "Your wife is restored by the touch of Rama's feet. Go to her. Take her back! Her heart is pure! She is blameless! Her soul did not sin."

Acceding to Viswamithra's wishes, Gautama went in search of Ahalya and accepted her back as his wife. Viswamithra, Rama, and Lakshmana bowed down to Gautama and left.

Eventually, they arrived at Sage Viswamithra's abode, and he said, "This is where I live. Under your protection against the evil that prevented me from doing my meditations, I will pray and perform my sacrifices."

More saints gathered together and made preparations for the sacrifice. The evil demons, including Thataka's sons, hovered above and tried to disturb the sacrifice by shrieking, throwing boulders, wielding their weapons, and generally causing confusion with magic. The saints were distraught.

Rama said, "Don't mind them! Go on with your prayers, and we will take care of them."

Lakshmana shot at the demons while Rama created a protective umbrella over the saints with his arrows. After the brothers attacked them, the demons fled. For six days, the princes watched over them and safeguarded them from the evil demons. Finally, the sacrifice was completed.

Sage Viswamithra said, "This sacrifice was performed for all humanity. Rama, only you could help me with this."

The next day, after morning prayers, Rama and Lakshmana asked the sage for further orders. Sage Viswamithra knew the purpose of Rama's birth. He thought of the service he still had to do for Rama—to introduce Rama to Sitha, the adopted daughter of King Janaka of the kingdom of Videha, and arrange for Rama's marriage to Sitha.

Viswamithra said, "You have accomplished much now. There is a great deal ahead for you. For the present, let us proceed toward Mithila City, where a great sacrifice is to be performed by King Janaka, and where many others will be arriving. You may enjoy this diversion."

Rama Strings the Bow

King Janaka, a close friend of King Dasaratha, ruled the kingdom of Videha from the city of Mithila. He was compassionate and brave, worthy to be Sitha's father.

Usually King Janaka personally plowed and leveled the chosen field for a sacrifice. As was his custom, many years ago he was plowing a field for his sacrifice. He saw a beautiful baby lying among the shrubs! The king was childless and accepted the baby as Goddess Earth's gift to him.

Carrying the baby in his arms, he went home and told his wife, "Here is a treasure for us. We shall make it our own."

She joyfully consented, and Janaka and his wife named the child Sitha and brought up this beautiful child as their own.

In those days, a teenage girl was considered marriageable. When Sitha became a teenager, King Janaka—though sad to part with her—tried hard to find a husband for her. But no suitor was good enough for Sitha!

Pleased with a sacrifice performed by Janaka a long time ago, Varuna, the lord of the ocean, had presented Janaka with Lord Shiva's bow and two quivers. It was an ancient, heavenly bow that an ordinary man could not pick up or move without help.

Knowing that only an exceptional man would succeed, Janaka said, "Sitha, my daughter, will be given in marriage to the prince who can lift, bend, and string the bow of Shiva that Varuna gave me."

Though many princes tried, none succeeded in winning Sitha in marriage.

Continuing their travel, Viswamithra, Rama, and Lakshmana finally reached the Ganges and bathed in the river. Refreshed, they proceeded to Mithila.

Silk flags decorated the city and fluttered in the breeze, as though beckoning Rama to come and wed Sitha.

After they crossed the moat surrounding Janaka's palace, they walked along the large main street. They heard the melodious singing of women, accompanied by harmonious sounds of the *veena* (a stringed, plucked musical instrument) and the beat of drums.

Beautiful young women were on swing sets fixed to trees outside, their colorful clothes fluttering with their movements as they swung and created a festive scene.

In addition to the blooms on the trees and the garlands worn by the women, flowers strewn on the street added even more fragrance. Shops heaped with exotic wares were visible as they walked past lotus ponds to reach the walls of the palace.

Suddenly, Rama, Lakshmana, and Viswamithra looked up as Sitha walked to the balcony to look out. Rama was awestruck. Mesmerized, he observed Princess Sitha playing with her companions on the balcony. He stood still, arrested by her beauty. She noticed him at the same time. Their eyes met in an endless moment as they captured each other's hearts.

Not long ago in Vaikunta (their original home in heaven), they had been together as Lord Vishnu and his wife, Lakshmi. In their present incarnation, being mortals, they did not recognize each other. They did not know they were incarnations of Vishnu and Lakshmi.

As Sitha watched Rama pass, she stood still as a statue, but as he left her sight, she furrowed her brow and wrung her hands. The rest of the day, she refused to eat, and as she looked outside, tears filled her eyes and slid down her cheeks, and she felt ill.

She said, "I feel strange. If the man I saw from the balcony does not attempt to bend the bow and succeed, I will kill myself! I will not marry any other man."

Her attendants were concerned. Bemused and overcome with feelings for Rama, she paced back and forth, confused and restless. Who was this man evoking such deep emotions in her?

Meanwhile …

Rama, in the seclusion of the guesthouse bedroom, brooded over the girl he had seen. Nothing indicated that she was a princess. He thought about her and wondered who she was. Her image burnt on his eyelids. Manmatha, the god of love, had done his work well! Rama tossed and turned and had little sleep.

The next morning, Rama and Lakshmana rose and went with their master to the ceremony at King Janaka's palace.

King Janaka saw the two brothers, and their beauty captivated him. He looked at them again more intently.

He said, "Who are these youngsters? Please tell me all about them."

"Warrior of warriors! The guests who have come here are no other than King Dasaratha's sons. They have finished partaking of your refreshments. Now they would be pleased to see the bow that you have from Lord Shiva and test its strength."

Sage Viswamithra continued to recount all the feats performed by Rama and Lakshmana, and King Janaka was impressed! He wished he could propose his daughter for Rama but knew he could not withdraw the condition made by him for a suitor to win Sitha's hand. He despaired of ever getting Sitha married!

King Janaka said, "Dear sage. What can I say to oppose what you are asking? All these years, many warriors have tried, but none could do anything with this magic bow. I am anxious at the thought of the bow being bent and my daughter, Sitha, getting married. If these young men can bend the bow, my anxiety will abate. My daughter would reap the rewards that she deserves for the good she has done in her previous birth."

The king ordered the bow wheeled in. When they saw the bow, the sage nodded to Rama to try it. With the greatest ease,

Rama swiftly picked up the heavy bow, rested one tip on his foot, and pulled the string toward him, tugging it taut, and bringing the tips together. When he increased the pressure on his grip, the bow arched, and everyone heard the deafening noise caused by the cracking of the bow at its arch.

The king was ecstatic and proclaimed, "My daughter, Sitha, will be given to Prince Rama in marriage."

The crowds in the palace and the city were jubilant and celebrated in the streets and in the countryside.

King Janaka sought Sage Viswamithra's advice on how to proceed with preparations for a wedding.

Sage Viswamithra advised, "First, send your fastest messengers to King Dasaratha in Ayodhya. Give the news to him and invite him."

Following the advice, King Janaka sent messengers to King Dasaratha bearing many gifts, news of all that had taken place, and—as fixed by astrologers and priests, based on the position of stars at a particular time—an auspicious time for the wedding. As was the custom, the bride had not been introduced to the bridegroom, and the parents made all the arrangements.

The Wedding

On receiving a message from King Janaka, King Dasaratha was overjoyed, especially when he heard of Rama's exploits, including the snapping of Shiva's bow. He made an announcement inviting all his subjects to Mithila for Rama's wedding.

Elephants, camels, carriages, and horses made their way with the masses from Ayodhya to Mithila. The line of movement was constant. The three queens came accompanied by thousands of ladies-in-waiting with their own entourage. Vasishtha, the chief mentor at the court, followed with two thousand Brahmins and priests. Rama's brothers, Bharatha and Sathurugna, came after.

The kings greeted each other, and King Janaka took King Dasaratha into his own carriage, and they entered the city together. Rama and Lakshmana were waiting to greet their father as he entered the city. King Dasaratha's heart swelled with pride when he saw his son Rama, who had matured and increased in stature. Dasaratha greeted his sons.

The wedding preparations were grand. Pavilions were set up for the guests. People came in from all parts of the world and were housed. Decorations and flowers were in abundance.

Elaborate preparations were made in the bride and bridegroom's houses. Delicacies and vast amounts of food were prepared for all. The citizen's partook of the celebrations with goodwill and gaiety. It was a wedding for the entire city!

The wedding day finally arrived. Sitha's hair was braided, intertwined with fragrant flowers. Precious stones, decorously placed in her long, black hair, glinted as they caught the light. Her handmaidens rubbed her body with aromatic fragrances and dressed her in fine silk. They frittered about excitedly, performing last-minute touches. She wore chains, diamond pendants, bangles, and ornaments on her forehead and nose. She was beautiful but had a heavy heart. She had decided that if the prince was not the person she had instantly fallen in love with, she would end her life.

Sitha went to meet her father and was escorted by him to the wedding hall. Her silver anklets tinkled with every step. They went in, and she stood demurely next to her father in the hall, eyes downcast, as was the custom. People gasped, amazed at her beauty.

Standing there, Sitha pretended to adjust her bangles, and through the corner of her eyes stole a glance at the bridegroom. Her heart skipped a beat, and she felt faint. She recognized him as the man down on the street, the one with whom she had fallen in love. He was so heartbreakingly handsome—even more than she could remember.

Rama looked intently at the bride and took a sharp breath. His heart filled with joy! Through all her finery, he saw the girl on the balcony! He realized that the beautiful, unforgettable girl on the balcony would soon be his wife!

The auspicious time for giving away the bride grew near. The drumbeats got louder.

At the appointed day and hour, King Janaka said to Rama, "Here is my daughter, Sitha, who will forever tread with you the path of duty! Take her hand in yours. Blessed and devoted, she will always walk with you, like your own shadow."

Accompanied by a crescendo of drumbeats, Rama accepted the chain that had been blessed during the ceremony, and at the auspicious time, he knotted it around the bride's neck. There was a hail of confetti and flowers from the onlookers. The pipes droned on, the drumbeats reached a climax, and Rama and Sitha became man and wife on earth.

King Janaka had helped find wives for Rama's three brothers in Mithila. They too were married at the same time.

After the wedding, Viswamithra returned Rama and Lakshmana to King Dasaratha and left to retire to the Himalayas.

King Dasaratha and his retinue returned to Ayodhya.

The people of Ayodhya were overjoyed and prepared the city for the return of the royals. Fragrant flowers gaily decorated the streets, and people thronged the streets to welcome the family back to their palace. The brothers entered the city of Ayodhya with their wives.

For twelve years, Rama and Sitha lived happily in Ayodhya.

Kooni's Treachery

King Dasaratha ruled Ayodhya faultlessly for a long time. One day he saw his reflection in the mirror, and seeing the gray in his hair, he realized he was getting old. The gray in his hair seemed to tell him that it was time to step down and relinquish the throne to his eldest son and live the remainder of his life as a Sadhu in prayer and meditation.

He loved all his sons but had a special affection for Rama. Rama deserved it for adhering to dharma (the righteousness he earned by behaving according to strict religious and social codes) and for his royal qualities.

Rama's physical, dark-skinned beauty, his strength, compassion, purity of heart, sweetness of speech to all, his statesmanship, and deep wisdom were admired by the citizens, who looked forward to him ascending to the throne.

King Dasaratha was happy that Rama was acceptable to all. He convened a meeting of all the ministers and leaders of neighboring lands and made his wishes known.

"I have performed my duty as king long enough; I have worked hard for the people. Now it is time to transfer this responsibility to my eldest son, Rama. As my ancestors did, I want to spend the rest of my days in the forest—in austerity. Rama is capable and ready to tackle the task of kingship. I can trust him to rule with valor and integrity. He will administer this office efficiently. I hope this distinguished assembly will permit me to give over the throne to Rama."

Shouts of joy rang through the assembly, and the leaders spoke in praise of Rama's virtues and his fitness to rule. The king was overjoyed! He turned to his chief ministers and bade them prepare for Rama's coronation.

King Dasaratha sent for Rama. Rama, followed by Lakshmana and Chief Minister Sumanthra, went to the king's palace. The king greeted Rama joyfully and hugged him to his chest.

After a few minutes, he let him go and said, "My dearest son! I am so very proud of you! I have one more duty for you to perform. I am now advanced in years. I cannot carry this burden any longer. Don't think that I am burdening you with this load. It is the duty of the son of royalty to remove the burden from the father's shoulders when the time is right. Wear the crown with pride and endeavor to perform your duty with compassion and attain goodness. This is what I ask of you."

Rama humbly bowed and said, "Be it joyful or sorrowful, I am duty bound to carry out your orders, whatever they be. As such, I will accept the kingdom and learn to rule it."

Dasaratha, overjoyed at his beloved son readily following his wishes, blessed Rama, hugged him tightly, and said, "You are a good prince, beloved by the people. Deal with absolute justice at all times. Humility, courtesy, consideration, and soft speech—there could be no limit to these virtues! There can be no place in your heart for lust, anger, or meanness."

The king sent invitations penned on gold leaf, *ola*, to all his ministers, requesting them to come to the palace.

He said to Sage Vasishtha, "Sage Vasishtha, make all preparations for the anointment of Rama. Do all the arrangements necessary for the coronation."

"It will be done as you wish!" Vasishtha joyfully replied. He then got into his chariot with his staff and left to start his work.

As soon as the ola was received by the neighboring kings, they arrived at the palace.

"Your Highnesses! I have thought to bestow my kingdom and all associated with it to Rama, as, according to past generations, this is his birthright," said Dasaratha.

The kings received this news with great joy.

"It is as it should be!" they said.

"It makes me happy to hear you say that! I am partial to Rama, but you are impartial. I wanted to hear your thoughts as to making Rama the next king. Are these your sincere feelings?" asked Dasaratha.

"Yes, Your Highness," they answered.

Rama returned to his palace and recounted all that had happened to Sitha. Even before he had finished, the king summoned Rama again to his presence.

Rama found the king anxious, and the king said, "I have premonitions that are frightening! Last night I had bad dreams! According to my horoscope, these are not good times for me. They even denote death! I would like the coronation to take place tomorrow! You must fast tonight—and tell Sitha to be prompt. The wife's participation in the ceremony is of the utmost importance!"

Rama listened intently, puzzled by the change of events. He promised his father he would follow all his instructions faithfully. Observing his son's puzzled countenance, the king finally explained.

"Bharatha is away at his grandparents' home right now. People can be fickle. I know he is devoted to you, but it is best we complete the anointing while he is away. He may ask why he was not made king. If you are already king, I am sure he will be delighted for you."

Though startled by his father's deviousness, Rama did not reveal his feelings. This worry about Bharatha on Dasaratha's part turned out to be a valid one.

Word travelled fast. Rama's mother, Kausalya, Sitha, and stepmother Sumithra heard the news and were overjoyed.

Rama went to see his mother, Kausalya, and received her blessings. People in the palace danced with joy as the news spread around.

Manthara, a deformed hunchback, was Queen Kaikeyi's favorite handmaid, and because she hunched, she was nicknamed

Kooni (the Tamil word for hunchback). All generally disliked her, but she especially disliked Rama. When he was little, Rama had made fun of her deformity and fired clay balls with his catapult at Kooni. She never forgave him.

When she heard of the forthcoming coronation set for the next morning, she thought she would get revenge on the prince. Under no circumstance did she want Rama to be king. She would advise King Dasaratha's favorite queen, Kaikeyi, and instigate some mischief.

Kooni hobbled down to Kaikeyi's chamber and found the queen resting. "Wake up, foolish woman, before you are ruined! You are betrayed and ruined!"

Kaikeyi opened her eyes and said, "Where have you been? What is the problem? Are you ill! Won't you call the physician and let him make it right?"

The clever Kooni said, "Destruction has struck both you and me, my girl! You still are beautiful and young—it holds your husband spellbound. Before time takes it away, get your husband to help you. The king has cheated you. Tomorrow he is crowning Rama as king and retiring."

Jumping up, Kaikeyi exclaimed, "This is great news! Thank you for bringing it to me! Here is your reward for the good news you bring!"

She took off her necklace and threw it on Kooni's lap.

Kooni cried out, "I said Rama is becoming the king of Ayodhya! You behave as if I had said that it was your son, Bharatha!"

She said, "I make no distinction between the two. It's all the same to me. Rama was the one born to it. I am a mother to Rama ..."

"You! Rama's mother?"

"Yes. Don't you know that one in Rama's position should count five mothers? The one who bore him, a father's sister, a stepmother, an elder brother's wife, and the wife of the guru - all these have equal rank as mother. Do you understand why I feel happy about Rama? I adore him! I am as much his mother as Kausalya! I am not a fool who doesn't understand things!"

Kooni beat her brow and wailed, "Do you not see the treachery around you? I feel sorry for you and the doom that hangs over you! You are too innocent ..."

All this talk made Kaikeyi receptive to what Kooni said next.

"Your husband is very cunning; he is capable of great cunning and trickery. You both are unequal. He is much older than you are."

"Why not? The king may have his own reasons. It makes no difference to me! Rama and Bharatha are the same to me!"

Since his first two wives had been childless, King Dasaratha, as according to custom, took a Kaikeyi as his third wife, hoping to continue his lineage. At that time, his queens had long been childless, and the king did not see a problem in agreeing to the condition for marriage Kaikeyi's father had made—that he would make the son born to Kaikeyi the next king! Many years later, after the great sacrifice, all three wives had sons. Rama was the oldest. Kaikeyi and Bharatha had never thought of or wished for the fulfillment of this old promise.

Kooni retorted, "People can change in an instant. Tomorrow at this time, he will be a different Rama. His only aim will be to rule for as long as he can. He will overcome all hurdles to achieve this. His biggest hurdle will be Bharatha, who may assert his claim at any time and win public support. Rama will banish him, break him down, or behead him. You and your husband will be ex-queen and ex-king with no power. You may even end up as Kausalya's handmaiden!"

"Never! She wouldn't dare! Let her try!" Kaikeyi was panic-stricken.

"Kausalya has always resented you because you were the king's favorite. She is no friend of yours. She will be a happy woman tomorrow and have the chance to wreak vengeance on you. Bharatha will always be a threat to Rama's throne. He will want him dead."

Kaikeyi's face flushed, and fear made her cling to Kooni.

Kooni decided it was time to bring out the remedy, so she said, "Do you remember King Dasaratha's war against Sambara in the south when you were with him? Dasaratha got wounded and lost consciousness. You drove his chariot skillfully away from the battlefield and gently removed the arrows from his body. You revived him! You saved his life! Did he not grant you two boons in gratitude? You may have forgotten, but you told me, and I have not! Ask for the two boons now! Demand that he should make Bharatha king instead of Rama, and for the second, ask him to banish Rama to the forest for fourteen years!

"Go! Lie in the sulking chamber," (a bedroom where the queen went when she did not get what she wanted), "and await the king! When he enters the chamber, do not look at him. Do not speak to him! The king will try to get around you. Do not yield! He loves you passionately and cannot endure your sorrow. He will give alternatives, but do not accept them. Do what I say! Do not be afraid! Unless Rama is sent to the forest, your wish will not be fulfilled!"

Kaikeyi's face shone with hope. "What a brain you have, Manthara! You have been the one to save me!"

"Remember what I have told you. Everything depends on how firm you can be. Victory is yours if you do not yield!"

Kaikeyi assured her she would do so, and removing her jewelry, she scattered them on the floor! She changed her finery for an old sari and lay on the floor in the sulking chamber.

Even without her ornaments and with her unhappy face, she looked distractingly beautiful.

King Dasaratha's Heartbreak

King Dasaratha entered Kaikeyi's residence with a beaming face to tell her the joyful news. Everything was going smoothly, and of all his queens, he sought Kaikeyi's company to relax and forget the cares of the state. She never interfered with his business and was always warmly welcoming. Today she was not in the usual places, and after asking, he finally found her in the sulking chamber.

The poor king found an unkempt, upset wife on the floor and tried to comfort her.

"Are you sick? Has something happened to hurt you? Has someone upset you? I will punish the person responsible for upsetting you," said the distraught king.

When all she did was sigh and not speak, he begged, "Tell me what's wrong! I will take care of it! If you want someone punished, I will do so. If you want someone released from prison, I will do so, even if it is a murderer. Ask me anything, and it will be done at once!"

Kaikeyi sat up and said, "Anything? No one hurt or dishonored me, but promise me you will grant me my wish, and I will tell you."

The unsuspecting, old king joyously said, "Tell me, Kaikeyi, and it will be done! I swear it! I swear it—on all I hold dear! On you! And on my beloved son Rama!"

She stood erect and in a firm voice said, "May the gods, the sun, moon, planets, and the five elements be witness to the commitment made by my husband, the king! He who has never broken a promise before has made one to me!"

Dasaratha said, "Tell me what you want."

Kaikeyi answered, "Do you remember the two boons that you promised me? In the battlefield? When you fainted? When I risked my life and saved yours, you said, 'Ask for two boons of your choice, and I will grant them to you.' Moreover, I said, 'I will wait to take them,' and you said, 'Whenever you want, even if it is a hundred years from now, I will give you whatever you wish.' Swear to me that you will give me whatever I want, or else leave me and let me die in peace!"

Dasaratha apprehensively said, "Let's go. Put on your fineries. Let us take a ride in the carriage around the city!"

Kaikeyi said, "Yes, in good time, after you have fulfilled your promise to me."

The king lost his courage and sensed impending doom at the mention of words such as boons, promise, and fulfill.

Kaikeyi continued, "You have promised me two boons and vowed it in the name of your darling son Rama. If you reject my demands, you will be the first of your lineage to go back on your word."

The king nervously said, "Ask for your two gifts. You shall have them now."

"Remember you have made a vow. You promised on your son Rama. I will now state my wishes. You have all the preparations made to coronate your son Rama. I would like you to coronate my son Bharatha instead, as my first boon. The second boon that I demand is that you banish Rama to the Dandaka Forest for fourteen years. Remember your vow. The good name of your dynasty is at stake."

The king took time to absorb this. He got up and blindly groped his way toward the couch. He felt faint.

"Is this a joke? Are you testing me?" he exclaimed in desperation. He closed his eyes.

Kaikeyi said relentlessly, "Send a message to get Bharatha back. He is quite far away. Give him time to get back and tell Rama to take himself away right now."

Dasaratha was thunderstruck! When realization hit home, he lost consciousness.

When he finally opened his eyes and saw Kaikeyi, he said, "You are a demon! What has Rama done to you to deserve this? Has he not looked upon you as a real mother? Are you trying to destroy my dynasty? You are like a venomous cobra!"

"Don't insult me, great king! Go to Kausalya. I never asked you to come to me—that is why I came to this chamber!"

The discussion continued through the night, and finally Dasaratha pleaded, "Coronate Bharatha but let Rama stay here. Bharatha is good. Let him be king, but let Rama stay in his own home! How can he live in the rough forest and make his home in the open, in the wilderness, with no shelter ..."

"He can! He is not the baby that you make him out to be! For fourteen years he must live away, wear the bark of trees, and eat roots and leaves ..."

The king screamed, "Do you want him to die?"

Kaikeyi said, "Don't be melodramatic! Either you keep your word or you don't! There is nothing more to discuss. If you don't keep your word, I will kill myself."

Regaining his senses, Dasaratha spoke in a low voice, "Kaikeyi, who has corrupted you? What evil has possessed you? Do you really think that Bharatha will agree to be king after sending his brother Rama to the forest? He never will, and you know it! What will the other kings of the world say? They will despise me for banishing my eldest son, who they think is the best of men, to the forest! Can Kausalya or I survive his banishment? Can King Janaka's only daughter bear to be parted from her husband? It will kill her to hear that he will be going to the forest for fourteen years! What a pity that my Bharatha should have such a monster for a mother! Kaikeyi, I beg you, on my knees, to have some pity on me!"

Kaikeyi cut him short and said, "Stop your drivel! Send for Rama and tell him to leave for the forest! Tell him the kingdom belongs to Bharatha. Don't waste time!"

The king said, "Very well. Let me see Rama's face once more before I die."

Saying this, he fell unconscious. They spent the night in silence, with Kaikeyi on the floor and the king on the couch.

The assembly room was crowding with dignitaries and public officials. Rama, after many spiritual baths and purification rituals as ordered by the chief priests, was dressed in simple silk and awaited the ceremonial robes.

A little before dawn, holy fires were lit, and the priests were chanting mantras. Music played from many sources. The public crowded in to watch the coronation. The atmosphere was merry and at the same time solemn.

The inner circle of ministers was concerned. The king had not arrived. Everything had to happen according to a timetable so that the coronation could happen at the auspicious time.

Usually, when the king spent the night with one of his wives, no one disturbed him. Eventually, the chief minister, Sumanthra, went looking for the king. He hesitated in front of the sulking chamber door and went in through the parted curtains. The sight that met his eyes startled him.

"Is His Majesty unwell? Has the food disagreed with you both?"

Sumanthra went to the couch and said softly, "Your Highness, they are waiting for you in the assembly hall. Are you ready to come?"

The king stirred and said, "Tell them all to go back. I have been tricked by a demon."

Kaikeyi said, "The king is incoherent. Go and send Rama here."

Sumanthra obeyed.

The Second Boon

Rama came in expecting to get a blessing from his stepmother. He touched his father's feet and did the same to his stepmother.

On seeing him, his father said, "Rama," and became speechless.

The king did not look into his eyes. Rama was bewildered!

"Mother, have I done something to offend my father? Did I not perform my duties properly? However angry he was, he would always speak sweetly to me. Is he sick? I cannot bear the suspense. Tell me, Mother!"

Kaikeyi seized the opportunity and said, "I will tell you. Your father is upset about hurting your feelings, but he made a promise, and he needs your help to fulfill it. He finds it difficult to tell you, so I will speak on his behalf. Your coronation will not take place today! It is your duty to help him and not ruin his reputation as an honorable and noble man."

She then explained the circumstances and the granting of the two boons. She also explained what the second boon entailed.

Rama was shocked but said quietly, "I will not fail my father. I have no desire to be king and no aversion to life in the forest for fourteen years. My only regret is that my father did not tell me this himself. I would have felt honored had he commanded me directly. I want you to make sure that he understands that I will gladly carry out his orders. I will take your order as his."

He moved closer to his father.

Kaikeyi said, "I will attend to him. You must remove yourself promptly. That's his wish."

Rama said, "Yes. I will do so. I will send for Bharatha."

Kaikeyi said, "No, no! I will handle everything. I will take care of Bharatha. You just quickly set out to the forest. That is your father's wish."

"I will bid my mother, Kausalya, farewell and leave at once," said Rama, and left.

Lakshmana had been waiting outside and heard everything. With eyes flashing with anger, he followed Rama. Rama went to Kausalya's quarters.

When Kausalya saw him, she said, "Why aren't you in your ceremonial robes?"

Rama replied only, "My father wishes to crown Bharatha."

Taken aback, Kausalya said, "Oh! But why?"

"For my own good. He has another command. He wants me to live with saints in the forest and derive all the benefit from their company."

Kausalya broke down and fell to the floor, sobbing. "What caused a father to give you such orders? What did you do?"

Rama and Lakshmana gently lifted Kausalya, and Rama said, "My father is renowned throughout the kingdom as an honorable man. He can't break his word. My brother will make a good king, and I will be fine in the forest. Don't be unhappy, Mother."

Lakshmana could not bear the sight of the queen's grief and said, "This king is old and lost his head over his young wife! Even the evilest are not punished to this extent. What did Rama do to deserve this? The doting, old man is not fit to be king. How can he listen to a woman and violate his duty? How can he send you to the forest and let your younger brother rule? The eldest should be the one to rule. The world will laugh at this absurdity. Don't consent to this. I have the power and the determination to overcome all opposition so that you can rule. In the face of these injustices, I must do my duty. Mother, now you will see the power of my arm!"

She said, "Rama, consider well what Lakshmana says. I can't say 'disobey your father,' so let me go with you. I cannot live without you! Don't go to the forest! If you leave, I will be here alone with your enemies!"

Rama replied, "Mother, let there be no talk of anyone going with me to the forest. Your place is with your husband. He looks unwell, and you have to care for him! Don't let him grieve for me; tell him fourteen years will fly by, and I will be back soon. My previous stay with Sage Viswamithra was beneficial and brought me countless blessings. Don't grieve for me!"

Rama then addressed Lakshmana and said, "Lakshmana! I know you are strong, but let's not disgrace our dynasty by misusing it. Aren't you my other self? Consider our father's condition. He is grief-stricken and cannot break his promise. We should not be angry with Kaikeyi either. We should not forget that she has been kind to us all these years. She is but a pawn in the hands of fate. Our little mother never showed any sign of evil all these years. Even sages have strayed. How can poor Kaikeyi withstand destiny? As long as our parents are alive, it is our duty to obey them! How can we insult our father, kill Bharatha, who is so dutiful, and expect to be happy in getting a kingship?"

Kausalya saw the fairness in what Rama said and gave him her blessing. She bade him obey his father's commands and come back glorious.

Rama smiled and said, "Don't worry, Mother. Fourteen years will pass by quickly."

Meanwhile …

Sitha was waiting for Rama to return in his ceremonial finery. She had not heard of the events taking place outside her chambers. She was surprised at his solemn face and asked him what was troubling him.

He explained all that had passed and said, "Princess, I know our parting will make us sad, but Janaka's daughter knows about duty! Take care of my father and the three queens. Mother Kausalya will need your support and guidance. Respect Bharatha as the ruler and don't offend him. Bharatha and Sathurugna are dear to me. Partake of the normal rites and rituals and be mindful of the feelings of others when speaking of me. Conduct yourself as befits your lineage. I will be leaving for the forest today."

She said, "A fine speech, my lord, but if you are so well versed in duty, you should know that a good wife shares her husband's troubles and that his duties are also hers. If Rama has to go to the forest, Sitha also is included. My parents have instructed me in my duties. I will go with you wherever you go. Do not think of me as obstinate. If you go now—I also go. I shall not be a burden. It will be a joyous holiday for us." Though she began the speech in anger, Sitha ended it sobbing. Rama's mothers and handmaidens cried at Sitha's plight.

Though he observed all this, Rama said, "Sitha! Coming to the jungle with me has many pitfalls. You have not considered this at all. That is why you so obstinately want to come with me. If you come with me, it will be an encumbrance for me. There are wild animals, and we have to live among them."

Rama tried to prevent Sitha from coming with him for her sake. Sitha did not understand this. She was hurt by his words.

She said, "Have you forgotten our marriage vows? Did we not promise to live together through thick and thin? You wish to leave me here so that you can live happily without me. All your problems are because of me. With you, I have nothing to fear; without you, I will wither and die! Living in the forest is difficult only for those that have no control over their senses. You and I can be masters of our senses. I implore you—parting from you is crueler than death."

Rama's love for her was as great as her love for him. Because he wanted it, and because he knew he could protect her, he agreed that Sitha would join him. She sent for the poor and gave away all her belongings in preparation for her life in the forest. Lakshmana also decided to join his brother to be of help to him in the forest and bade his wife good-bye. The three went to bid the king good-bye.

The king had aged and looked shrunken. He went with outstretched arms to greet Rama and fell in a heap, feeling faint. Lakshmana and Rama lifted him up tenderly and asked for his blessings.

The king said, "My word binds me, but why don't you brush me aside and seize the kingdom by force?"

Rama replied, "I have no wish for power or desire the kingdom, Father. I have set my heart on going to the forest."

"Don't be troubled by the thought that you may be doing me wrong. Send for Bharatha and fulfill your promise to mother Kaikeyi. Give him your blessing, and cast aside your grief. I will be fine! If I got all the wealth in the world but broke your promise I would be unhappy. I will be back in fourteen years in time to do my duties for you. Sitha and Lakshmana are also going with me. Please bless us, Father."

The King said, "Go and come back safely. Make our lineage proud. Be dutiful and firm in resolution. Where can a father find a son like you? I did not intend that this should happen to you."

Kaikeyi provided the three with clothes made of dried, tree bark that looked like mesh. They dressed themselves, and were ready to depart. Rama begged his father to be attentive of his mother, and listen to her, as she was only staying to take care of the King. He said he did not want her to die of sadness, and wanted her to be there when he came back.

Lakshmana touched his mother, Sumithra's, feet and said, "Mother."

His mother said, "I am proud of your devotion to your brother, Rama. It is your duty to protect and help him. Be vigilant and guard him. Your elder brother is your protector, and your King! It is the duty of our race! In the forest, regard Rama as your father and Sitha as me. Go cheerfully, my son and god be with you."

With this, they departed.

King Dasaratha lay prostrate with grief. When he was able to, he got out of Kaikeyi's chamber.

He watched the dust of the chariot as it left for the forest, taking Rama, Sitha and Lakshmana. When it was out of sight, he fell to the ground moaning. Kausalya and Kaikeyi sat on either side of him.

The King said to Kaikeyi, "Do not touch me, you sinful woman! Everything is over between us! If Bharatha accepts your offer, he does not need to perform my final rites. May you live a happy widow!"

Thus, the King lamented, and went to Kausalya's chamber to lie down - and await death. The grieving Kausalya did her best to console the King.

Sumithra, seeing the sorrowing Kausalya, said to her, "Sister! You should be proud of Rama for his virtue and honor. You are blessed among women for having a son who scorned a Kingdom to live in the forest to uphold his father's honor! We should not feel sorrow for a son who walks in the path of his ancestors, and wins undying fame. I am proud of Lakshmana for accompanying his brother, and admire Sitha for not forsaking her husband despite the hardship of following him into the forest. This is no time to feel sorrow – Rama's virtue will protect them from evil!"

Exile to the Forest

Rama, Sitha and Lakshmana, went to bid goodbye to Sage Vasishtha. They fell at his feet and he blessed them. As the rose with their meager belongings and gladly departed for fourteen years to the forest his eyes filled with tears. Sumanthra, the chief minister, requested them to get into the chariot that he brought. The chariot would drop them at the edge of the forest. Sad and tear-filled crowds were milling around them. Some of them followed the chariot as it went on toward the jungle. As they travelled on in silence darkness fell. They stopped for the night in a beautiful orchard, and except for Rama, Sitha, Lakshmana and Sumanthra all found some place to rest their heads for the night.

As soon as Rama observed that the others had fallen asleep he called Sumanthra over and said, "Sumanthra, I know that these people have great love for me and it would be difficult to tell them to go back. For us to leave without sending them back would not be good. Therefore, you take the chariot back without us and our followers would return to Ayodhya happily thinking we have returned."

Sumanthra sobbed uncontrollably and with tearful eyes said, "Lord, how can I go back alone? While you are walking over pebbles and rough terrain, how will I go back in the chariot in comfort? What will I tell the people? Will I tell them that I abandoned our lord in the jungle and came back? What will I tell the King? If I tell him I just left you in the forest I will have to watch him wither and die. Queen Kaikeyi only made him grieve I will help *Yama* (the God of Death) kill him. Oh my god…"

Sumanthra fell to the ground writhing in agony.

Rama gently lifted him to his feet and said, "Whenever we are born in this world, we have to learn to treat happiness and grief as one. You understand this. You are unhappy that I have to stay away but if I go back and make you happy would I not be at fault for breaking my father's word? Have you forgotten that would be against *Dharma*? If in this life you live according to Dharma then you will be happy and in your next life you will reap the rewards. The same way that we rejoice when we follow Dharma and the results give us happiness we must rejoice when the results give us sorrow. Can we abandon Dharma when we find it brings unhappiness to us? It is not your right to oppose me when I am trying to follow Dharma – you should encourage me. You will do the following."

"Go first to Sage Viswamithra and tell him that I am very happy and that we are going to the forest. Go with him and tell my father that I was not at all worried about going to the forest. Tell him: 'He is sure that this will only bring him good fortune.

His wish is that you have the same love for Queen Kaikeyi that you have for him. He also wishes that you would deal lovingly toward Bharatha. The fourteen years will pass by very quickly. He says he will come back and worship once more at your feet.' This was the message that I want you to give the King. After that, you will go to the queens and give them my loving wishes. You will tell them that I wish for them to take good care of the king. He is sorrowful now and needs their help at all times. You, too - stay by the king's side and give him your support and help."

Sumanthra, comforted by Rama's words took leave of him and prepared his departure.

He asked Sitha, "Do you wish to send any messages through me, my lady?"

Sitha replied, "First, convey my respects to the King and then please check on the birds I brought up and make sure they are well cared for."

Sumanthra then turned to Lakshmana and asked, "Do you wish me to convey anything?"

Lakshmana replied with mounting anger, "Sumanthra, should I send my respects to Dasaratha, who after promising Rama the kingdom gave it instead to Kaikeyi? Yes – tell him that Rama eats roots in the jungle and sleeps on the ground – while he, though he has the title of being a compassionate ruler enjoys the best of meals and luxuries! Tell my brother, Bharatha, that he coveted what should rightfully belong to Rama! I do not accept Bharatha as my brother anymore. Tell him this!"

Hearing this Rama chided his brother and said, "Brother, it is not right that you say these things. In future please don't speak like this."

At dawn, when everyone was asleep, Rama, Lakshmana and Sitha bade farewell to Sumanthra and, after Rama and Lakshmana got their locks matted with the milk of the Banyan tree, they walked away. Sumanthra watched them and slowly turned the chariot back to the palace.

The crowds woke up and finding Rama missing followed the track of the chariot back - thinking that Rama had changed his mind and returned to the palace.

Death of a King

A sad Sumanthra went back to the palace and found the streets desolate. He stopped in front of Dasaratha's palace and went in. He found the king more dead than alive in Queen Kausalya's chamber where she was tending to the king. In low tones, he repeated Rama's message to the king. As she heard Rama's message, an anguished Kausalya begged Sumanthra to take her, and leave her with Sitha.

Sumanthra said, "Queen, be brave. Rama and Sitha are happier than they would be in Ayodhya, and Lakshmana is happy in the service of the brother he loves."

To Dasaratha, agonizing in his bed of pain, Kausalya spoke words of reproach. The stinging words caused more pain to the King.

"You have kept your word, and made Kaikeyi happy. What about the others? Here I am, without the love of my lord, or the sight of my son. Are you not delighted with what you have done? It is enough that you make Kaikeyi and Bharatha happy. You need not fear that Rama will interfere with Bharatha's Kingdom - even when he returns after fourteen years."

The king turned to his wife, with a humble prayer for forgiveness, "Have pity on me, Kausalya. You have been kind and forgiving to strangers. Be compassionate toward your husband who has always loved and honored you and whose heart is breaking with sadness."

Seeing her husband in such dire straits, the generous queen fell to her knees and begged his forgiveness.

Time dragged on, and Dasaratha said to Kausalya, "Are you still here, my dear? Kausalya, I do not see you. All is over. Will Rama come? The light is fading! Ah, Kausalya! Oh, Sumithra!"

That night, while his fatigued queens were sleeping, and unbeknown to anyone, King Dasaratha's life slowly ebbed away.

Bharatha Returns to Ayodhya

Dasaratha's death left the kingdom without a ruler. The funeral would be after Bharatha returned. The palace dispatched messengers to the house of the parents of Kaikeyi, requesting Bharatha to return to Ayodhya. When Bharatha and Sathurugna arrived in Ayodhya and found the city deserted, they rode directly to Dasaratha's palace but did not find the king there.

A maid told Bharatha that his mother wanted to see him, and he immediately went to his mother's apartment. Kaikeyi inquired after her family, and when Bharatha informed her that all was well, he asked after his father.

Calmly, Kaikeyi said, "Your father has passed away. He is happy and at peace now."

Bharatha exclaimed loudly, "Only you could be so callous! Is your heart made of stone? The world has never seen a greater ruler or a nobler father. What a time to be away!"

He was in deep thought and then said, "Until I see and speak to Rama, my grief will be unbearable."

In a matter-of-fact voice, Kaikeyi said, "Rama, Lakshmana, and Sitha have gone to the forest."

Bharatha was dumbfounded.

"What sin did Rama do to deserve this penance? Why did he have to go to the forest? Who sent him away?"

Kaikeyi decided to tell Bharatha the truth. She said, "Rama committed no crime. While preparations were being made for his coronation, I asked the king to grant me the two boons he had promised me. For your sake, I asked that he crown you king and send Rama to the forest. Bound by his past promise, the king agreed, and Rama, Sitha, and Lakshmana left for the forest. Your father couldn't bear the parting and died of grief. Do not be sorrowful now. You know your duty. Bear your burden of kingship. You should receive the fruits of my action in the spirit in which I acted. Perform the last rites for your father and accept your responsibilities."

Bharatha felt unbearable grief for his father's death. His love for his brother, Rama's exile, concern for his mothers, Kausalya and Sumithra, who might die without their beloved husband and children, caused him pain. He also felt shame for what his mother had done for his sake.

"Banish Rama indeed! Murderer of my father! You are a demon! How could you have banished the only child of mother Kausalya? I shall perform the last rites and go look for Rama in the forest, fall at his feet, and beg him to come back and be crowned! Did you think that you and I could be happy with all this misery you have caused?"

Bharatha rushed from his mother's palace, intent upon meeting Kausalya and Sumithra to beg their forgiveness and mercy. He was surprised to find them already on their way to see him.

As they met, Kausalya said, "Bharatha, the kingship, secured by Kaikeyi, awaits you. Take it, and may all happiness be yours."

Bharatha was desolate and said, "Mother, why do you torture me thus? I am innocent. I knew nothing of the wicked things going on here. Don't you know of the love I bear Rama? Do you think I would wish such misfortune on him? I have no desire to benefit from or have anything to do with this!"

He fell at Kausalya's feet.

Kausalya tenderly lifted him and said, "My dear son, my grief is doubled by seeing the suffering in your innocent heart! Our fate is such, my child. May the rewards of goodness come to you!"

She embraced him.

BOOK 2

Rama

In Exile

Guha Meets Rama

Rama, Sitha and Lakshmana journeyed on and set up camp for the night on the banks of the Ganges.

Guha was the chieftain of thousands of tribes living on the banks of the Ganges. He was a hunter king with a pack of dogs who lived many years by the river and had a fleet of boats. He was an excellent marksman and had a large army. A dark, stocky, older person with large feet covered by leather, he never smiled, and his eyes were filled with anger.

Overjoyed at hearing that Rama was in the vicinity, he very humbly set out to greet him. Leaving aside his spear and his sword, and asking his followers to wait, he went to Rama's abode.

Finding the entrance open and feeling it was wrong to enter without permission he said, loudly for all inside to hear, "Lord! I am like a dog but have come to obey your commands."

Hearing this Lakshmana came to the entrance. He saw Guha who stood in reverence.

"Who are you? Why did you come here?" he asked.

"Lord, I am but lower than a dog. I make a living off the river. My name is Guha. I came to worship at the feet of Lord Rama," Guha replied.

Lakshmana said, "Is that so? Wait here and I will be back."

He went inside and said to Rama, "Master, there is a man who seems pure of heart. His name is Guha and he is a hunter. He makes his living off the river and wishes to see you."

Rama was happy to meet Guha and said, "Good! Bring this Guha to see me."

Lakshmana took Guha to meet Rama. Guha saw Rama, and his angry eyes filled with love. Overjoyed at seeing Rama's countenance filled with love and compassion, he fell at Rama's feet and worshiped him. He stood up and waited reverently on the side.

Rama said, "Guha we are delighted to meet you. Sit."

Guha did not feel comfortable to sit in the presence of one so great and refused. Instead he said, "Oh great one! I brought you a meal of fish and honey."

Rama replied, "You have brought this food with faith and devotion. Due to certain circumstances, we cannot partake of the meal, but please accept my heartfelt thanks and consider it eaten. I am sorry that we are in this state. We intend staying here tonight. If you could, please go home and return early tomorrow to help us cross the river."

Guha replied, "Though I regret leaving you, I will do what you say and come back to help you."

Rama said, "Guha, if you wish, you could stay the night with us."

Guha was delighted. He and his followers immediately started protecting Rama. He noticed that Lakshmana was with him and asked him why they were in this predicament. Lakshmana told him everything.

Guha admired and loved the Royal family, and offered his best hospitality to Rama.

Rama said, "Guha, I could spend fourteen years enjoying your hospitality, but would that be fulfilling my vow? We have to live on fruits, roots and permissible kinds of meat such as we offer in the sacrificial fires."

Lakshmana made a bed of grass for Rama and Sitha, and kept watch with Sumanthra and Guha while the others slept.

Guha said to Lakshmana, "Brother, my men are keeping watch, and I myself am not sleeping. There is a bed made for you. Go get some rest."

Lakshmana said, "How can I sleep, Guha? Here lying on the ground is Sitha, daughter of the great Janaka, and daughter-in-law of the great Dasaratha. I wonder how Ayodhya is bearing this! My mother and mother Kausalya must be wailing, or I doubt if they are alive. My father had sufficient strength to tell Rama to go to the forest, but I doubt if he survived his actual departure! He must have passed away, depriving us of performing the last rites for him! In any case, it is very unlikely we will see our mothers when we return to Ayodhya after fourteen years."

As Lakshmana spoke in sorrow, Guha was in tears.

Next morning, with Guha's help, Rama, Lakshmana, and Sitha went by boat to the far bank of the Ganges. Clusters of bamboo grew on the shores, and the leaves rustled as the mighty river moved on timelessly. There was a rough track in the midst of an overgrown forest. Here they stood, alone together for the first time.

Rama said, "Lakshmana! You lead, Sitha will go behind you, and I will follow. Spare Sitha as much of the hardships of forest life as possible."

After walking awhile, Rama said, "Lakshmana! Should you not go back to Ayodhya to care for our father and mothers?"

Lakshmana replied, "Forgive me, brother, but I will not return to Ayodhya."

They followed the track until dusk and looked for an appropriate resting place. They found a banyan tree and spent the night under it. The tree was old and large, a splendid specimen with prop roots growing down around to help support the heavy branches of the tree—forming a natural enclosure.

In the morning, they left to find the home of the Sage Bharathuwasa. He would be the best person to direct them to a safe and comfortable part of the forest for their exile. They saw the mountains in the distance and thought they would reach their intended destination. Hearing that they were approaching, Sage Bharathuwasa went with heartfelt gladness to greet them and invite them to his abode.

The sage was a pious, loving man who had read the scriptures thoroughly. He wore robes made of tree roots. He trod very slowly and was careful not to step on the smallest of insects along his path. Seeing Rama, he was distressed at the attire of the future king.

He said with tear-filled eyes, "Customarily, kings have come to visit the sages after bestowing their kingdom to their children, but you are here at a very young age. Is there a reason for this visit?"

Rama told his story to the sage.

After hearing the story, the sage said, "Oh my god! Do these things happen even at this age? It must be the sins of the previous birth!"

He thought, *Imagine my friend King Dasaratha's grief to have given the kingdom to his firstborn—only to take it away and banish him to the forest. After saying this, how will he continue living? This must be retribution for sins that the king committed. There is no point worrying about it.* He pacified himself and went forward to invite Rama, Sitha, and Lakshmana to his ashram for simple refreshments of sweet fruits and nuts.

At sunset, they partook of his hospitality. The sage treated them as if they were his own children, with affection and consideration. Rama asked him where they could spend fourteen years quietly in the forest.

Sage Bharathuwasa said, "My Prince, I wish to tell you about this place. We have plenty of water, flowers, fruits, and edible roots and tubers. Living here banishes evil and multiplies blessings. Therefore, I suggest you live here with me. This is a good place for anyone trying to meditate. This is where the Ganges, Saruya River, and Yamuna meet. This is why I am reluctant to leave this place. It is not easy to find such a place. Please stay here."

Rama replied, "This is not close to Kosala but also not too far. So if the people from Kosala hear that we are living here, they will come here in droves. That is why we don't wish to stay here. Great sage! Please tell us of a place where we could live in peace."

"What you say is true. If you travel past the orchard that is a distance away from here, you will get to Chithrakoota hill. It is a beautiful place and the appropriate place for you to live. May you find peace there."

With his blessings, they made their way to Chithrakoota hill.

Following the directions given by the sage, they came upon the river Kaalindi. They put together a bamboo raft and crossed the river.

After resting under another banyan tree, Rama and Lakshmana hunted. They mostly subsisted on meat—venison, jungle fowl mostly—and fish. Kshastriyas, the second of the four castes, were omnivorous. Rama belonged to the Kshastriya caste and lived in the jungle in the Kshastriya way.

In the distance, they saw the Chithrakoota hill and walked briskly toward it. The forest had beautiful flowers and edible fruits. The variety of flowers, fruits, and creepers growing profusely and climbing large trees astounded Sitha. Rama pointed out the edible fruits and provided them for her to eat. The water running through was clear and fresh. They were sure they could live happily in these surroundings. Sitha was fascinated, and Rama took delight in sharing these moments with her.

Lakshmana, a smart worker, soon built a hut and made it waterproof, comfortable, and convenient. After building a skeletal structure of the roof using bamboo wood, he wove palm fronds and used these to construct the roof. He made the walls with bamboo leaves and held them in place by ropes made of coconut husk. Then he covered the leaves with mud. He built a raised platform with wood, stone, and mud for the floor, and he paved the floor with a mixture of mud and cow dung. The cow dung also acted as an antiseptic. The floor dried quickly. He even made a door and windows.

Overcome by the results, Rama praised his brother profusely.

He said, "Sitha's feet walking through the forest was a wonder, but, Lakshmana, your artisanship and the resulting cottage built with bamboo and material from the jungle is a miracle!"

Distressed that his brother was sleeping outside on the ground while he and his wife were in the cottage built by Lakshmana, Rama said, "Brother, I came to the forest because of the promise made by father, but you did not have to come here and undergo all this hardship."

Lakshmana replied, "Brother, I hate to see you worrying about my comfort. I don't think it is right. I delight in serving you and don't have any problems in doing so. So please don't worry about me."

With Lakshmana and Sitha by his side, Rama lacked nothing. The grandeur of the mountain scenery and the birds singing their sweet songs in the forest with the sounds of the river flowing close by pleased his heart. They would sometimes go to the river and, among the lotuses in the sand hillocks, watch the swans playing.

Though it was a hard life, the three young people forgot they were in exile and lived there happily carrying out their devotional routine and sharing the chores.

Bharatha Seeks Rama

Meanwhile, back in Ayodhya, after a few days of mourning for King Dasaratha, Vasishtha and the assembly of learned men addressed Bharatha and said, "In the absence of the king, Rama, and Lakshmana, we feel the time has come for you to assume the rule of this kingdom. You are also a rightful descendant from the same ancestors and are next in line for the throne."

Bharatha surprised and delighted the assembly by saying, "It is not right for me to rule the kingdom that rightfully belongs to the eldest son, my brother Rama. I will find him and beg him to return home."

With this, Bharatha, his three mothers, and an army of workers and followers to help clear the forest set out to find Rama. They travelled for days through the jungle and arrived at the river Ganges.

Gazing across the Ganges, the hunter king, Guha, saw the commotion across the river. He saw Bharatha, his mothers, and his followers crossing the river in boats.

When he realized it was Rama's brother Bharatha, he went to meet him with courtesy and gifts. Bharatha and his large army were camped there, prompting Guha to ask Bharatha whether he had hostile feelings toward Rama.

Poor Bharatha was so pained that Rama's friends thought he would hurt Rama.

He said, "Have no fear, Guha! I have come to beg Rama to return with me, to rule over Ayodhya as king."

The overjoyed Guha said, "My lord, who in this world could renounce such wealth and power? Who could make such a sacrifice and come, unsought, to give all this to him? Your glory will shine forever!"

Guha bowed to Queen Kausalya and asked Bharatha, "Brother, who is this with you?"

Bharatha replied, "This is King Dasaratha's First Lady, the great lady who bore Sri Rama. She who was supposed to live in the lap of luxury, but due to the misfortune of my birth, she gave up everything to follow me and look for Rama."

Guha was saddened by the humble appearance of Rama's mother and worshiped her. Kausalya found out from Bharatha about Guha and liked him.

Deciding to lessen their grief, she approached Bharatha and Guha and said, "Children, don't be sad. Rama and Lakshmana met such a good friend only because he came to the jungle. Together with this mighty Guha, the five of you will be able to safeguard this wide world."

Guha was then introduced to Queen Sumithra, and he bowed to her.

Then Bharatha introduced Kaikeyi and said, "She is the one who brought us all these troubles. She imparted grief even to me—the one who is from her womb. She is the only one who is not grieving. This is the one who bore me!"

Guha acknowledged Kaikeyi as a mother and worshipped her.

Guha proceeded to provide all the help Bharatha needed to meet with Rama. Bharatha set forth toward Chithrakoota where Rama was camping. He wore bark and went on foot, just as Rama had done before him.

Finally, after travelling for days, they saw a column of smoke from Rama's ashram and cheered. Bharatha left his followers behind and approached Rama with Vasishtha and Sumanthra.

Lakshmana heard the loud noises and commotion and saw the army and crowds on the horizon. He climbed a hilltop and looked out. Seeing Bharatha and his followers, he concluded that he had come to kill Rama and make sure he had the kingdom more than fourteen years. Angrily, Lakshmana scrambled down the hill and ran to Rama.

Approaching Rama, Lakshmana said, "Brother, Bharatha has no respect for you! That is why he has come here with a large army to wage war against you!"

Lakshmana armed himself and prepared for war.

He fell at Rama's feet and worshiped him. Then heading in the direction of Bharatha, he said, "Brother, though born after you, I will singlehandedly destroy Bharatha and his army!"

Hearing Lakshmana's angry words, Rama, wishing to calm him, said, "Lakshmana, you have lost your temper in vain. Do you think that anyone from our family would go against our creed and behave dishonorably? Bharatha would never do anything against our religion. His code of behavior is according to the writings that are for all the world to obey. It is best for you to think that Bharatha comes here in love and to give me the kingdom. For you to think otherwise is ugly and unbecoming. For you to say this is not right. Bharatha is merciful and honorable and one to do what is right. You will see this in a little while."

Leaving his army behind, Bharatha approached Rama with his brother, his palms together worshipfully over his head and tears pouring down his cheeks. Rama saw the dusty appearance of Bharatha and looked at him from head to toe.

Then looking at Lakshmana, Rama said mockingly, "Brother, look at the war armor that Bharatha has on!"

Lakshmana felt ashamed and sad. His anger evaporated as he looked at Bharatha.

Bharatha begged Rama's forgiveness and flung himself down at his feet. He felt as though he was standing in front of his dead father and was happy.

He said, "Brother, because of my mother's boons, you have lost a kingdom and been banished to the forest. I have given up looking for happiness and have betrayed our creed. I have been the cause for dethroning the rightful heir."

Rama lifted him up gently with many kind words.

He said, "My brother Bharatha, come. Why are you so sad? How is my father?"

"Brother, due to being parted from you and because of my mother's devilish ways, our father has departed from this world."

Rama felt like a firebrand had been applied to an open wound. He reeled in shock, and overcome with grief, he fell to the ground in a faint.

After a few moments, he regained consciousness and, realizing that his father was gone, started sobbing and cried, "Father, the light of my life, the righteous ruler who was mightier than a lion. I thought of getting the kingdom, and you died because of me! You wished to give up the kingdom and wanted to go and meditate—is this what you wanted? Did you think I would rule after I killed you? You have departed this earth with all the strength, valor, nobility, compassion, and wisdom and left us here."

Seeing Rama's grief, his three brothers went to him and with great affection held him. The sages and the ministers tried to comfort him with words of wisdom. Rama heard all but grieved silently.

According to the Bhagavad Gita, Hindu scripture, the soul is a spirit and cannot be destroyed. It is free, unbounded, holy, pure, and perfect. The Hindu's goal is to avoid reincarnation so that the individual soul merges with the supreme soul and achieves liberation.

Seeing Rama still grieving, Sage Vasishtha said, "Our bodies are as unstable as drops of water. There is no point in grieving over the loss of this. There is no point in crying. Instead, with your hands pour the water to cleanse your father's soul of all his sins."

The sage's words comforted Rama. He went with him to the river. After getting into the waters of the Ganges, Rama returned. Sage Vasishtha gave him the words from the scriptures and instructed him in performing the funeral rites of the son for his father, praying and chanting on the banks of the Ganges. Rama and his entourage of ministers, elders, and sages then returned to the ashram where Sitha awaited them.

On seeing Sitha, who should have been in the palace surrounded by her ladies-in-waiting and decked in fineries and jewels, Bharatha was moved to tears and cried unashamedly.

Affectionately hugging Bharatha, Rama chokingly said, "Sitha, your loving father-in-law passed away, as he could not bear the long separation from me."

Sitha was shocked. She fell down and wept profusely. The women gently led her away to the river to bathe, and after finishing, returned her to Rama.

Sumanthra brought the three mothers and presented them to Rama.

Rama looked at his three mothers and said, "Mothers, where is my father now? Tell me," and he wept at their feet.

All the queens were so affected by this that they wailed loudly. The onlookers joined in the sadness.

The next day, Rama said, "Bharatha, the ruler of Kosala is dead. Now, as he ordained, you have to accept the crown and rule the kingdom. Why are you dressed in these clothes? What is the reason for this? Tell me!"

Bharatha said, "Brother, I am here with all these people to beg you to come back and be our king."

Rama replied, "Yes, fourteen years from now! That was our father's wish. You are king now by our father's authority. There are no words higher than that of a father, and we will obey. You have all the good qualities necessary to rule. Therefore, you will rule Ayodhya!"

The argument went on, and finally Bharatha said, "Rama, I shall rule for fourteen years and not a day more! If you don't return at that time, I shall set myself on fire. Give me your sandals, and I shall rule on behalf of that symbol. I will not reenter Ayodhya until you return, but rule from just outside the city."

Bharatha went back with Rama's sandals in his hands. He set himself up in a little village called Nandigram on the outskirts of Ayodhya, installed Rama's sandals on the throne, and ruled the country as regent.

After Bharatha's departure, Rama, Sitha, and Lakshmana left the beautiful hut Lakshmana had built in Chithrakoota and went north, deeper into the jungle so that those wanting him to return to Ayodhya could not easily find him. They encountered many sages, and among these were Sage Athri and his wife, Anusuya.

The sage and his wife affectionately welcomed them, saying, "Children of the great king! Your appearance here is as though you have come with all the gods and all the heavens! What miracle did I do to deserve this?"

Rama, Lakshmana, and Sitha stayed at the sage's ashram at his request that night. Sitha, with her wifely virtues, won the heart of the saintly Anusuya, who insisted that Sitha should have all her jewelry and fineries and that she should wear them. Sitha reluctantly agreed and looked even more beautiful with the jewelry and silks. The next day, they departed from the ashram and continued their journey.

Viraathan Encounter

Rama and his companions continued through the jungle. Soon they saw a Rakshasa with long, rust-colored ringlets travelling fast. He was clad in tiger skins and other animal skins. Resting on his large shoulders were many necklaces of tigers intertwined by pythons. Even as he traveled, he kept eating elephant meat hungrily.

He stopped blocking their path. Rama and Lakshmana, not realizing who he was, teasingly asked him to move. The Rakshasa felt humiliated and grew angry.

He shouted, "Just wait! Just you wait!"

In a trice, he scooped up Sitha in one arm and rose up in his chariot.

Rama and Lakshmana grew angry and shouted, "Hey! Where do you think you are going? Come back!"

The Rakshasa laughed and shouted, "Hey! Thanks to a wish granted by the gods, nobody can kill me! I am the great Viraathan! Even the whole world together cannot kill me! I will give you one chance and allow you to live! Just be on your way as the Sadhus you are dressed up to be, and I will make this woman my wife!

Rama and Lakshmana followed Viraathan's chariot and prepared for battle.

Rama said, "He does not realize our prowess at war! That is why he is blabbering so!"

The brothers started shooting arrows at the various weapons—including his famous trident and uprooted hills and trees—that Viraathan aimed at them. Rama sent his arrow, and it made a resounding war cry. Viraathan, startled by the war cry, dropped Sitha.

After a fierce battle, Viraathan finally fell down at Rama's feet, badly hurt. Though the brothers tried, they could not kill the Rakshasa. Then Rama suggested to Lakshmana to make a big pit so that Viraathan could be buried alive.

After Lakshmana dug the pit, Rama kicked Viraathan's body into the grave with his foot. In that instant, Viraathan transformed from a frightful Rakshasa to a new being remembering everything from his previous birth! He emerged from the pit discarding his Rakshasa appearance and as the handsome celestial being he used to be! His anger had dissipated, and his face looked calm and pleasant. He recovered his more saintly ways. He truly knew who Rama was, and his heart overflowed! He knelt at Rama's feet, praising Rama in song and telling him the story of his curse.

He was a celestial being named Tumburu in his former life. Once, in a fit of lust, he had embraced Rambha, the heavenly nymph, while she was dancing. For this transgression, Kubaran, the head of the celestial beings, cursed him birth as a Rakshasa. The curse would lift when Rama's feet touched him.

Viraathan said, "Ignorant as I was, I did not know right from wrong! I killed and ate everything that came my way! In my ignorance, I caused you pain in many ways! Please forgive me!"

Rama blessed Tumburu. Tumburu bowed to each of them and bade them good-bye and left the earth. Rama, Sitha, and Lakshmana moved on until they reached a cluster of ashrams. Here they rested all afternoon.

Sage Sarabhanga's Suicide

The sun started its descent, and the northern wind helped cool the day. Rama, Sitha, and Lakshmana continued their journey. They reached Sage Sarabhanga's ashram, which was surrounded by beautiful *kungumam* (red powder made from saffron or turmeric, used in Hindu and social markings) trees that provided abundant shade.

Rama sensed something amiss in the ashram. He heard voices inside.

A voice like that of a god said, "Oh bountiful Sage Sarabhanga! Due to your diligent prayers and penance, Brahma decided that you should be invited to the heavens now. He has given you this prestigious invitation, and if you accept, someone will be sent to get you."

A man's voice replied, "My Lord Indra! I do not want rewards for my meditations and prayers. It is not right for you to demean me by offering to take me to heaven as reward for my sincere prayers. Only those going to heaven can be reborn. What is the point in my returning after all the penance I have already done?"

Rama then looked at the chariot near the ashram and recognized it as belonging to the god Indra. Rama asked his brother and wife to go away from the ashram. Known for his greatness and valor, Rama entered the ashram.

Indra was on his way out of the ashram and with his thousand eyes looked intently at Rama. He bowed his head at seeing Rama's state.

He said, "What could we do for the one who is going to save us? Aren't you the one who is destroying those that would harm us? Are you not the one who created that sin? You were the one who taught me the right way when I was in a trance and helped me overcome it."

He worshiped him and, with Rama's blessings, left for the heavens.

On seeing Rama, Sage Sarabhanga fell at his feet, worshiped him, and pleaded with him to bring his wife and brother and stay with him. Rama went out and brought back his wife and brother and accepted the sage's hospitality.

At the crack of dawn, the sage lit the fire for prayers and approached Rama.

He said, "My lord! Please give me your blessings to leave."

"What is this? What are you trying to do?" asked Rama.

"Great one! I wish to immolate myself and ascend to heaven with your blessings! Seeing you is fulfilling one of my goals! I refused Brahma's invitation because I wanted a higher, everlasting world where there is no time or change. Having attained my last goal on earth, I have no reason to be on earth. Please grant me permission to die in your presence."

Saying this, the sage and his wife walked into the fire and entered heaven. Rama, Lakshmana, and Sitha were depressed by the event. They left the holy abode of the sage and continued their journey.

The three travelers moved on past hills, melodious streams, and beautiful trees. They passed black rock paths and groves and met the men and women of tribes and the sages who lived there. They all greeted Rama, Sitha, and Lakshmana joyously. The sages set up an abode for the travelers and provided whatever comforts they could. Later, the sages told them of the continued harassment by the Rakshasas.

Rama said, "Good Sadhus and great men! Wherever the Rakshasa hide—whichever world—I promise I will destroy them or be destroyed by them! You do not deserve this punishment. I will save you from this! Even Rakshasas protected by Shiva or any of the other gods—those who do not deal with mercy and kindness will be opposed by me! Do not fear!"

The sages implored Rama to live among them and spend the years in exile with them. Rama, Lakshmana, and Sitha settled there to be of help to the sages against the Rakshasas who lived there.

Ten years passed …

Sage Ahathi

Finally, after staying with the sages at their request, Rama got their blessings to move on. Accompanied by his wife and brother, Rama walked a very long way through jungles and narrow paths and finally reached Sage Sutheeshnan's ashram.

They were greeted with joy, and the Sage said, "Please stay here with us."

The travelers fell at his feet and worshipped him. They accepted his invitation and decided to stay with him.

The sage said, "God of mercy! What penance did I do to deserve this good fortune?"

Rama said, "I have one thing to ask of you. I have a yearning to see Sage Ahathi. Could you direct me to him?"

"Good thinking! We decided to tell you the same thing! You can go to Sage Ahathi's ashram and meet the great sage. You will find out whatever is necessary. He has been expecting your arrival. He will be delighted to see you! It is good for the gods and mankind."

The sage directed them to Sage Ahathi's ashram, blessed them, and sent them on their way.

They passed many gardens and streams and met up with the sage who greeted them with tears of joy! He invited them to stay at his ashram, but Rama refused.

"If I live here and keep my word to the Rishis to kill the Rakshasas who persecute them, I will defile the sanctity of your ashram and bring dishonor. Therefore, as the Rakshasas come from the south, I think I will go south and live there. What are your wishes?"

Sage Ahathi said, "Good thinking! Please accept this arrow that belonged to MahaVishnu. Also, this mighty sword and Siva's bow that he used to destroy the *Tripurasua* (three flying mountain kingdoms)."

Rama graciously accepted the gifts.

The sage said, "Rama! On the wide beaches of the Godavari River, there is a place called Panchavati. That will suit your needs perfectly as a place to live. There is no shortage of water or food there. There are even swans that will delight Sitha and while away the time. Go there; it is the perfect place for you!"

Rama, Sitha, and Lakshmana took leave of the sage and joyously set out south to Panchavati.

Meeting with Jatayu

They proceeded south over hills and across streams for a long time. At a distance on the top of a hill, they saw a beautiful sight. It was a large eagle with its wings spread out and shining like the rays of the sun! His red claws set off the colorful picture. He was holy, learned, honest, faultless, farseeing, and deep thinking. He had been the vanquisher of evil Rakshasas and was respected and admired.

They climbed the summit and approached the great eagle. They were unsure whether this was a Rakshasa in disguise. King Jatayu, the great eagle, also had misgivings. Uncertain of their identities, he said, "Who are you?"

They replied, "We are King Dasaratha's children."

"Children of the great king? Your appearance here is as though you have come here with all the gods and all the heavens! What wonders did I do to deserve this?"

The Great Eagle, Jatayu, explained to Rama, "I am a great friend of Dasaratha. I am a divine being in eagle form. King Dasaratha and I were so close that Dasaratha, on the battlefields, remarked, 'You are the soul, I am the body. We are one!' How is my friend?"

Rama was overjoyed to meet one of his father's friends. He told him of King Dasaratha's death. When Jatayu learned of Dasaratha's death, he broke down and cried—and fainted. Rama and Lakshmana revived him with their tears, and he regained consciousness.

After mourning his friend's death, Jatayu bade them follow in his shadow as he flew, leading them to the banks of Godavari. The forest was beautiful. They saw deer, bison, bears, and elephants drinking from the river at various points, flowering creepers on trees, and blue water lilies floating in the ponds. They heard chirping birds and the rustle of leaves among the old trees.

Bunches of lotus blossoms lifted their heads as Rama, Sitha, and Lakshmana approached, but the Godavari River rushed past the lotuses, making them lose their petals, which the river gathered and deposited at the feet of the trio. It appeared as though the river behaved like a father joyful to see his favored children!

After Jatayu safely escorted them to their destination, he flew back to his perch and from there continued to keep a watchful eye on them as if they were his fledglings.

Rama and Sitha rested by the banks and enjoyed the river. They lost themselves in their love and daydreaming.

Rama called his brother and, pointing, said, "You will build our home here."

Lakshmana went ahead and built a house made of mud, thatch leaves, and wood, enclosed with a fence affording privacy and protection from the elements. Rama was delighted with his brother's skills and entered his new home with wonder.

Sitha, Rama, and Lakshmana made this home and lived there happily. Rama never forgot his promise to protect the good souls from the Rakshasas and their Chief Ravana, to establish peace in the region.

Soorpanakha Meets Rama

One morning, as customary, Sitha, Rama, and Lakshmana went to bathe in the Godavari River. They returned to their home, and after completing their duties, they sat around speaking wistfully of the old days.

Suddenly, there appeared a Rakshasas woman with rusty brown hair who had been wandering around the forest, where she lived alone. She was horribly ugly but had the magic power to assume any form at will. Rama's good looks immediately enamored her, and she desired him.

She went toward Rama in her natural ugly form and asked, "Who are you? What are you doing in the forest belonging to the Rakshasas?"

In those days, it was customary for the person accosted to introduce himself.

Therefore, Rama said, "I am Rama, the eldest son of the great King Dasaratha. Meet my brother, Lakshmana, and my wife, Sitha. I am here at the request made by my parents to fulfill dharma. Now, please could you tell us who you are?"

"Have you heard of Ravana, the heroic son of Visravas and the king of the Rakshasas? I am his sister. My name is Soorpanakha. My brothers Kumbhakarna and Vibishana are also great warriors. The lords of this area, Kara and Dooshana, are also my brothers. I am not under their control but a free person. Everyone in this region is afraid of me! The moment I set eyes on you, I fell in love with you. Why are you wandering around with this midget of a woman? Come with me! We can wander the forest at will! I can take any shape I want. Don't worry about this woman. I will eat her up in a trice!"

Amazed and amused, Rama said, "Oh beautiful one! Your love for me will end in trouble for you. I am here with my wife and do not wish to have two wives, but my brother is as good looking and is the proper husband for you. Leave me alone."

Rama was sure that Lakshmana could deal with Soorpanakha.

Soorpanakha turned to Lakshmana, who played along and said, "Don't let him fool you! He is trying to cheat you! I am here as a slave to my brother. You deserve more than that! You are a princess! Don't mind Sitha. Soon he will prefer you to her!"

She turned around back to Rama and said, "It is this wretched insect that stands between you and me! How could you love this skinny girl without a waist? I will finish her off!"

Soorpanakha sprang at Sitha.

Rama intervened just in time to save Sitha and shouted at Lakshmana, "Attend to this monster and teach her a lesson!"

Lakshmana promptly drew his sword and cut off her nose and ears, thus maiming Soorpanakha. She ran off howling into the forest.

Yelling in pain, she went in search of her brother Kara and threw herself at his feet and sobbed out her story. It was a blow to the Rakshasas!

She said, "Look at me! They are still roaming in your domain, and you do nothing!"

Kara replied, "Calm down and tell me everything. I will punish those who have dared do this to you."

After obtaining the relevant details, he sent his generals to kill them and bring their lifeless bodies back. He ordered them to bring Sitha alive.

It did not take long for Rama to vanquish the generals.

Soorpanakha went back to Kara, who was shocked to find out what had happened. Kara went with an army led by Dooshana to battle with Rama.

Rama saw their approach and said, "Lakshmana! Take Sitha and go to a cave in the hills and keep her safe!"

After they left, Rama, dressed in armor, faced the Rakshasas army and sent arrows flying in all directions, slaying chariots and soldiers. Dooshana himself was now in front of Rama and rushed him. Rama slew him, and he fell dead like a big monster.

Finally, after a mighty battle, Rama killed Kara and all the Rakshasas!

Lakshmana and Sitha returned from the cave and rejoiced that Rama singlehandedly defeated the Rakshasas army.

Soorpanakha, watching from afar, took a moment to grieve her brothers and left for Lanka to convey the news of their brothers' demise and their armies' annihilation to her brother Ravana.

Ravana

King Ravana, the god of three worlds, was in his palace in Lanka surrounded by courtiers and attendants. The kings of the earth he had vanquished stood around with arms upraised in an attitude of servitude. Beautiful maidens from around the world sang and danced and ministered to his every wish as admirers showered him with flowers.

Ravana was the head of the Rakshasas. He had ten heads borne on twenty muscular shoulders. His mouths were cavernous and had mustaches. He held himself erect. No one could fathom where he was looking with his ten heads.

He had enslaved gods to perform menial tasks. Vayu, the god of wind, was blowing away the faded flowers and garlands; Yama, the god of death, was employed to sound the gong to tell the time of day. Agni, the god of fire, was in charge of illumination and kept lamps and incense lit. Sage Natarajan played soothing music on the veena.

Soorpanakha entered the palace alone, screaming wildly and holding her bleeding nose to face Ravana.

She dashed up and fell before Ravana's throne, shouting, "See what happened to me!"

When Ravana saw her mangled face and the state she was in, he thundered, "Who did this to you?"

She said, "I cannot describe the beauty and grandeur of this being! His strength is unmatched. He singlehandedly destroyed our army!" She went on to explain in detail all that had happened, including the deaths of Kara and Dooshana.

Ravana said, "Tell me—why did he do this to you? How did you provoke him?"

Soorpanakha said, "He has a woman who should be yours! The whole earth has no one to equal her beauty! If you win her, you will throw out all your current favorites! You will be her ardent devotee. Her name is Sitha. Overcome by her beauty, I waited and watched, trying to snatch her away to bring back to you as a present! That was when this man's brother fell on me and slashed my face!"

Ravana said, "Tell me all about her …"

Soorpanakha described Sitha in detail, from head to toe. Ravana fell madly in love with the image her words conjured up. Every word that she uttered gave him pleasure and pain.

She said, "Set forth and capture Sitha! When you have captured her, you keep the woman and give me Rama. I will deal with him."

Ravana felt uneasy. He held his ten heads erect and left the hall, his mind seething with ideas for abducting Sitha. He ignored his wives. He was obsessing over the image of Sitha. He sent for his sister.

She said, "Go fetch Sitha! She is yours! Is there anything you can't get? She is waiting for you."

Soorpanakha's plan was working.

Ravana went in search of his uncle Mareecha. He went straight to his dwelling and explained what had happened.
He said, "I want to avenge my brother's death and my sister's disfigurement. I want to carry off Rama's wife, Sitha. I need your advice and help."

Mareecha, who had firsthand knowledge of Rama's powers, cringed at the words. He tried to dissuade Ravana. He said, "Whoever gave you this advice of carrying off Sitha wishes the end of the Rakshasas race! Don't you have a happy home and devoted wives? Return to them and live in prosperity. To hanker after Rama's wife is the destruction of the Rakshasas race."

Ravana said, "To disgrace and punish this Rama is a duty I owe to my race! There is no equal to you for skill and magic powers. Here is what I want you to do for me. I want you to turn yourself into a golden deer and prance in front of Sitha near Rama's ashram. She will insist on Rama and Lakshmana pursuing and capturing you. Meanwhile, when she is alone, I will capture her and carry her off. Rama will despair and be most vulnerable, pining for his beautiful wife! At that time, it will be easy to kill Rama and avenge our race."

Mareecha, stricken, knew exactly what would happen.

He said, "I have listened, my king, to all that you have said. You were not told the truth. Rama is a dutiful son, not a criminal! He is a mighty warrior who excels in the use of arms. Don't make Rama an enemy and bring ruin to the Rakshasas. You will destroy the race of Rakshasas—and Lanka itself! Rama is the first among mortal men. How dare you cast longing eyes on Sitha? You will burn and be reduced to ashes if you approach the blazing fire of Janaka's daughter. Don't fall prey to Rama's shafts. Do not seek your own death!"

"I am king! I have come to tell you I have decided to do this! I seek your advice, and it is your duty to obey me. I want you to turn into a stag, lure Rama away, and when you are far enough away, shout, 'Ah, Sitha! Ah, Lakshmana!' Hearing this, Sitha will conclude that Rama is in trouble and force Lakshmana to go to his aid. When she is alone, I shall take her off to Lanka. Once you perform this service, you are free to do as you like! If you do not help, your life is at stake!"

Mareecha thought to himself, *It is better to be killed by a foe than family*, and so he agreed to help.

Mareecha and Ravana traveled over hills and cities, rivers and kingdoms, to the Dandaka Forest. Here they saw Rama's ashram in the clearing and climbed out. Ravana bade Mareecha carry out his part while he stayed out of sight.

Mareecha transformed himself into a beautiful, golden deer and frolicked near the ashram. Sitha, who was gathering flowers, watched, enthralled at the deer's beauty. She wanted to own the golden stag! She called Rama and Lakshmana to come see it.

"Let's go see it," Rama said indulgently.

He could never refuse his wife anything. They came out, and Lakshmana grew suspicious. *A stag with a body of gold, legs, and jeweled tail—yet it leaps?* Lakshmana felt that this was a Rakshasa in disguise. Rama and Lakshmana were aware that Mareecha would take the form of a deer to lure hunters who came into the forest and kill them.

Sitha wanted Rama to catch the deer so that she could have it as a pet and later take it back to Ayodhya. Rama refused to go after the deer because he was wary. Sitha begged and pleaded; she wanted, at least, to take back the beautiful skin. Eventually, he asked Lakshmana to go after the stag.

Sitha said, "You don't want to get this for your wife?"

Sitha stalked off into her home in a temper. Rama knew that Sitha was sulking because she wanted her husband to get the deer for her. Reluctantly, Rama agreed to kill the deer and bring the skin back to Sitha.

He said, "Take care of Sitha, Lakshmana. Guard her safely— be vigilant! I will be back with the deer—dead or alive! If this is a Rakshasa, what does it matter? Stag or Rakshasa, it is all the same."

Rama set off with his bow and arrows.

Mareecha led Rama away from his home and tried to give Ravana enough time to carry out his plan to abduct Sitha. When he was far enough away, Rama, tired of the pursuit, sent an arrow piercing the stag.

Mareecha knew the end was near.

As the arrow hit him, he assumed his natural body, imitated Rama's voice, and called out, "Ah, Sitha! Ah, Lakshmana!" and fell dead.

Sitha, hearing this, said, "Something has happened to my lord! Lakshmana! Go and help him!"

Lakshmana replied, "No harm can befall Rama. It is a Rakshasa trying to deceive you."

Again, Sitha heard a cry. This time, Ravana imitated Rama. "Alas, alas, ah, Sitha! Ah, Lakshmana!"

Sitha was in agony.

She said, "Lakshmana, this is not the time for explanations or speculations! Go and help him!"

Lakshmana did not stir but tried to calm Sitha.

"Rama is the best warrior in the world, and no one can destroy him! This is a trick! Don't worry," Lakshmana said.

She lashed out at him with cruel words and accused him of being a traitor.

She said, "I know what you are planning! You always planned to let Rama die! You are scheming to keep me for yourself!"

Lakshmana shut out Sitha's words and tried to obey his brother's command, but finally, when Sitha threatened to set fire to herself, he relented.

He reluctantly set off, saying, "May the gods protect you. Our elder Jatayu is there to watch us and guard you."

Sitha Meets Ravana

The moment Lakshmana left, Ravana appeared in the garb of a *sannyasi* (a hermit)—old, lean, with a staff and a begging bowl in his hands.

He said, "Who is there? Is anyone in to welcome a sannyasi?"

Sitha heard the trembling, old voice and opened the door.

Seeing the old man, she said, "You are welcome, sir. What do you want? Where do you come from?"

Ravana was overwhelmed at the vision before him. Sitha was even more breathtaking than his sister's description of her.

His mind was racing, and he thought, *I will obey her every command. I will do nothing else in life except enjoy her company. I will make her the queen of my empire. I will reward my dear sister for this!*

Eating the fruits and berries given by Sitha, he started praising Sitha's beauty. Sitha was uncomfortable and started to look toward the entrance, hoping to see the princes.

Ravana began praising himself. "A favorite of Lord Shiva himself, all the gods wait to do his slightest bidding ..." He continued to extol Ravana in the third person, describing his wealth and power.

Puzzled, Sitha said, "Why should a saintly one as you choose to live in this Rakshasa country?"

Ravana replied, "Rakshasas can be good to those who are good to them. Since they are the most powerful in the world, why not live in harmony with them?"

Sitha said, "My husband has vanquished Kara, Dooshana, and their armies. His mission is to rid this world of them and establish peace on earth."

Ravana was getting angry. He said, "Wait until you see the mighty Ravana with his twenty shoulders! No human can kill him!"

Sitha said, "What if he has twenty shoulders? Didn't Parasurama, with two shoulders, once imprison him until he cried for mercy?"

This further angered Ravana, and he started losing his saintly disguise. Sitha watched the transformation, terrified.

Ravana said, "I would have crushed and eaten you, except you are a woman, and I want you and will die if I don't have you! My ten heads have not bowed down for any god in any world, but I will take off my crowns and touch your feet with my brow! Only be my queen and command me what to do!"

Sitha covered her ears and said, "How dare you! If you wish to save your life, run and hide before Rama returns!"

Ravana said, "Rama's arrows can't touch me. Have mercy! Be kind to me! I am dying for your love! I will give you a position greater than a goddess can have! I prostrate myself before you!"

When Ravana fell to the floor, Sitha recoiled and cried, "Oh my lord! Oh, brother Lakshmana! Come and help me!"

Ravana, remembering an ancient curse (cast on him by his nephew Nalakuvara when he raped his wife, Rambha) that if he touched any woman without her consent, his head would explode, and he would die instantly, dug the ground under Sitha's feet, lifted it off with her, placed it in his chariot, and sped away. Sitha fainted.

When Sitha revived, she tried to jump out of the chariot. She called to the birds and the animals to report her plight to Rama, and finally, she cursed Ravana.

He only laughed at her.

"You think too highly of Rama! He is a mere human being, and it is beneath my dignity to fight humans!"

"Ah, yes, your class is ashamed to mix with humans, but you do not think twice about coveting and attacking a helpless woman! Rakshasas like you do not know what is right and what is wrong. If you have the courage to face my husband, stop the chariot immediately!"

At this moment, Ravana felt an obstruction in the course of his flight. Jatayu, the great eagle who had promised to guard the children of Dasaratha, had noticed Sitha's plight and hurled himself at Ravana with all his might! The wind caused by the flapping of his mighty wings uprooted trees, elephants, and all other animals, and they swirled before the chariot and disrupted its flight. Before the battle started, Jatayu appealed to Ravana to release Sitha and just go away.

Jatayu advised him, "Don't seek the ruin of your whole clan, class, and tribe! Rama's arrows will be your undoing."

"Stop your chattering, you senile old bird! Let all those heroes come! I will deal with them. She will go with me."

Jatayu started attacking the chariot and Ravana. He flapped his great wings and paralyzed the chariot. He hit and tore with his body, beak, and claws. Ravana parried and hit, using all the weapons in his command, but Jatayu was unrelenting.

Finally, Ravana pulled out a special sword—gifted to him by Shiva—and dealt a final blow to Jatayu, cutting off his wings and piercing his throat. The great, noble bird fell to the ground.

After Jatayu fell, Ravana left the chariot and carried Sitha with the ground beneath her on his shoulder. Exercising his power to fly, he carried her off to Lanka. As Ravana took her away, Sitha bundled her jewelry and threw it down, hoping that Rama would follow it and find her.

Many hours later, Ravana entered the city of Lanka. He installed the grief-stricken Sitha in the inner apartment of his palace.

Summoning some Rakshasas, he ordered, "Let no one approach her! Give her whatever she wants—jewels, clothes, gold ... Serve her and honor her as you would me! Anyone who offends her will be killed!"

Sitha did not know where she was or how far from Rama. The Rakshasas took Sitha to Asoka Vana, a beautiful park attached to the women's apartments. The Rakshasas kept her prisoner here. The park was a grove of asoka trees and called Asoka Vatika (or Asoka Vana). Though the trees were in blossom, and the fragrant flowers and trickling spring could have lifted the spirit of almost anyone, Sitha remained distraught. Yet she still had faith in Rama and Lakshmana. She was sure that they would find her and kill Ravana, and they would return to live happily in their ashram.

The Death of Jatayu

Following his sister-in-law's stern commands, Lakshmana went in search of Rama. He was happy to find him well and anxiously hurrying toward the hut.

Rama hugged Lakshmana tightly and said, "Why did you come here, brother?"

Lakshmana replied, "Sitha was convinced that you were crying for help and insisted I go to help you. I told her it was not your voice, but she would not believe me. Though I tried hard to convince her, she wanted me to find you. She threatened to jump in the fire if I did not obey her. She didn't stop with that but started a fire. That is why I had to come looking for you."

Rama said, "You are not to blame for leaving Sitha alone. I did not listen to you when you tried to tell me that the deer was a fake. I only heard Sitha imploring me to get her what she wanted. I think the Rakshasas are intent on evil."

They hurried to their hut, and Rama felt as if his soul had left him. The hut was empty!

Lakshmana said, "We found the chariot tracks and the place where earth was removed in order to abduct Sitha. It is fruitless to stand here and worry like weaklings. Before the chariot with Sitha and the earth travels too far, we should go find it."

As Lakshmana waited respectfully, Rama said, "Let's do as you suggest."

They traveled north and came upon Ravana's shredded flag with the veena. At first they thought the gods had intervened on Sitha's behalf and fought, but then they realized that Jatayu had torn the flag.

They hurried on and found the arrow that Jatayu had damaged. They followed the trail left by damaged arrows, dead horses, and precious metal vases and utensils.

They finally found Jatayu, who, with the greatest effort, had stayed alive until Rama and Lakshmana came that way in search of Sitha. Lakshmana poured water over Jatayu's face and revived him. With eyes filled with tears, they embraced him. Jatayu opened his eyes and was happy to see Rama and Lakshmana.

Lakshmana recounted all that had happened with the golden deer until the present.

With his dying breath, Jatayu gave an account of what he had witnessed and how Ravana had lifted Sitha with the soil and gone.

He was sad that he did not know where they went and said, "Do not despair. You will succeed in the end."

The great Jatayu then died.

Meeting with Hanuman

Rama and Lakshmana considered Jatayu a second father and assembled a funeral pyre and performed the funeral rights for him.

After the funeral, they continued their search for Sitha. Following Sitha's trail by hearsay and hints, they traveled further south and entered the outskirts of Kiskinda.

A giant monkey race populated Kiskinda, and Vali ruled this kingdom. The giant monkeys were intelligent, strong, noble, and of godly parentage. Whatever their form and shape, when they spoke or acted, their physical appearance went unnoticed. The companion and helper for Sugreeva, Vali's brother, was Hanuman.

While keeping watch for intruders, Hanuman observed Rama and Lakshmana entering Kiskinda. He assumed the form of a young scholar and hid behind a tree in their path, trying to figure out whether they were ascetics carrying enormous bows on their shoulders or warriors dressed in tree bark, with matted hair, parading as ascetics.

Hanuman stepped up before them and announced, "I am the son of Vayu and Anjana. My name is Anjaneya or Hanuman. I am in the service of my chief, Sugreeva, the son of the sun god. I welcome you to our kingdom on his behalf."

Rama whispered to his brother, "Don't be fooled by his appearance. Though he looks like a youthful scholar, he must possess great powers."

Addressing Hanuman, he said, "Please lead us to your chief."

Hanuman replied, "Whom shall I have the honor of announcing?"

"We are the sons of Dasaratha, the late king of Ayodhya ..." Rama told him of the events that led to their being in the forest and not in the palace, and explained why they were here.

On hearing the story, Hanuman prostrated himself at the feet of Rama.

Rama said, "No, no! You are a man of learning, and I am only a warrior. You should not touch my feet!"

Hanuman replied, "I only assumed the guise of a scholar to come before you." He resumed his real body and stature of a giant monkey! He then left them and returned with Sugreeva.

Rama felt an instinctive compassion for Sugreeva and, sensing this, mentioned his difficulties in a general way. They cut down a branch of a tree and sat on it, engaged in cheerful conversation.

Hanuman and Lakshmana did the same on another branch. As a result of this talk, Lakshmana felt a deep affection for Hanuman.

He said to Hanuman, "My brother is the eldest and left his kingdom and came to the forest. Here, his wife—dearer to him than life—was abducted by Ravana, who tricked and lured us far away from our ashram. We seek Sugreeva's help to rescue and recover her. We freed Kabandha, a cursed celestial being, and before he ascended to the heavens, he told Rama, 'Go to Rishyamooka Hill and find Sugreeva. He is hiding in fear of his brother Vali. Gain his friendship, and he will help you find Sitha.' So we are here, seeking the friendship of your chief."

On the other log, Sugreeva told Rama, "Through no fault of mine, I am deprived of the necessities of life and in exile."

Rama asked, "Have you lost your home, and are you separated from your wife?"

Sugreeva, too overcome to reply to this question, remained silent. Hanuman stood up and told them Sugreeva's story.

Sugreeva's Story

Hanuman said, "In ancient times, using Mount Meru as a churning rod, the gods and demons tried to churn the ocean to obtain nectar. They were unable to move the churner. Vali, the brother of Sugreeva, possesses unlimited power. When appealed to by the gods, he pushed aside everyone and turned the churner, obtaining nectar. The gods consumed the nectar, and it saved them from death. They rewarded Vali with unlimited power and empowered him to cross the seven oceans with one stride. They also enabled him to gain half the strength of anyone who approached and fought him, thus augmenting his powers. All nature feared him! Every day, Vali visited all eight directions and worshipped Shiva.

"Vali is Sugreeva's older brother. He is our king and is supreme. Sugreeva was his next in authority. Under his rule, we were all happy. One night, a Rakshasa named Mayavi came to the gates of Kiskinda and challenged Vali to a fight. Vali was not one to refuse and rushed forward, followed by Sugreeva. Suddenly, Mayavi realized he had been rash and fled into the hills. They saw him disappear into the mouth of the cave, and Vali followed him.

"He instructed Sugreeva, 'Stay here at the mouth of the cave and wait until I return!'

"Sugreeva waited for a long time, but Vali never came out of the cave. Instead, he heard indistinct shouts and groans that sounded like Vali's. Subsequently, he saw blood gushing out of the crevice.

"He waited for days, but Vali did not return. He decided to go into the cave in search of Vali, but his councilors, the elders around him, dissuaded him, saying that Vali must have perished. They blocked the entrance, posted guards, and left.

"The elders presumed Vali dead. Since Kiskinda could not be without a ruler, they managed to persuade Sugreeva to take the throne. Sugreeva was the new ruler of Kiskinda.

"Eventually, it was not Mayavi but Vali who came out of the cave! He found the entrance blocked and jumped to the conclusion that Sugreeva had trapped him in the cave. Enraged, he kicked the entrance open and rushed out like a tornado to the palace. Sugreeva stood up to greet his brother, overjoyed at seeing him alive, but Vali did not give him the opportunity.

"Haggard with rage and wounds, he exploded, 'You tried to bury me alive!' and he boxed and pounded his brother in the presence of the elders and councilors.

"Sugreeva tried to explain but did not get a chance. Sugreeva managed to break free and ran away, pursued by Vali. Sugreeva ran to Mount Matanga, where he sought refuge.

"Sage Matanga had laid a curse on Vali for something bad he had done. The curse was that if Vali ever set foot on Mount Matanga he would lose all his power, and his skull would explode. Vali swore to kill Sugreeva if he ever set foot outside the mountain. He then returned to his throne, which he had not lost, took Sugreeva's wife as his own, and continued to rule. Sugreeva had lost his wife and his home."

Rama, moved by this story, said, "Certainly I will help! Tell me what you want."

Sugreeva answered, "For fear of Vali, I live here in the forest. I would like you to kill Vali and restore to me my kingdom and my wife."

Sugreeva took Hanuman aside and asked him, "What are your thoughts on his offer to help?"

Hanuman replied, "I have no doubt that Rama can kill Vali. My inner voice tells me he is Vishnu himself. I notice that he has the marks of the conch and the disc in his palm. Who else could break the bow of Shiva? Who else could have ousted Thataka? Who else could have revived Ahalya?

"When I was young, my father, Vayu Bhagavan, commanded me, 'You shall dedicate your life to the services of Vishnu!'

"'How shall I know him?' I asked.

"'You will find him wherever evil is rampant, trying to destroy it. When you meet him, you will be filled with love and will not be able to move away from his presence.'

"I have no doubts about him, but if you wish, test him. Tell him to shoot his arrow at the trunk of a tree. If the shaft pierces and goes through, you can be sure it will be able to kill Vali."

They went back to Rama, and Sugreeva asked him to give them proof of his archery.

Rama smiled and said, "Yes, if it will help you. Show me the trees."

They took them to seven ancient trees that practically reached the heavens. Their trunks were huge. Rama took his arrow and shot not only one but all seven trees, the seven seas, the seven worlds, and all things in seven, and then the arrow returned to its starting point in the quiver! Sugreeva was overwhelmed. He was sure he was in the presence of a savior. Rama noticed a heap of bleached bones at the top of the mountain and asked Sugreeva about it. Sugreeva told him the story.

Dundubi's Story

Sugreeva said, "These are the bones of a monster, a powerful demon in the shape of a buffalo, named Dundubi. He was strong and arrogant about his invincible power. Wishing to prove himself, he searched out Vishnu and challenged him to war. Vishnu directed him to Shiva. He travelled to Kailaya Mountain, and with his mighty horns he attacked the Kailaya Mountain and shook it!

"Shiva appeared before him and said, 'What is it you want? Tell me!'

"Dundubi replied, 'I want to battle with you forever! This is my wish!'

"Shiva said, 'Against your strength and power I cannot fight! Go to the gods!'

"Dundubi went in search of the gods and started challenging them. The chief of the gods, Indra, approached him and said, 'If you want to fight for a long time, don't wait here. Go find Vali, the appropriate one for war.'

"Accepting the advice, Dundubi went down to earth and came into this region. Here he shouted foul challenges to Vali.

120

Vali, who could never resist a fight, came up and started fighting Dundubi.

"They fought for over a year, and finally Vali broke Dundubi's horn off his head and gored him to death with it. He then picked Dundubi up by his neck, whirled him about, and hurled him into the air. Dundubi's body fell to earth here on Mount Matanga, where Sage Matanga was performing some sacred rites. The sage moved off after putting a curse on Vali for defiling his prayer ground. This evil kept Vali away from this mountain."

Rama ordered Lakshmana to push away the bones, and the site returned to its former state of sanctity and beauty.

Vali

Sugreeva said to Rama, "I have heard of all your troubles from Lakshmana. Wherever she is, we will help find Sitha soon. Sometime ago, attracted by screams, we looked up. My companion and I saw a Rakshasa carrying a weeping woman and speeding fast across the sky. She was crying, 'Oh, Rama! Oh, Lakshmana!' As we looked up, she too saw us. She removed her scarf, tied her jewels in it, and threw down the little bundle. We picked it up and put it safely away. See if the jewels are Sitha's."

On hearing this, Rama shouted excitedly, "Fetch it! Fetch the bundle!"

They brought the bundle, and when Rama saw the scarf, he was beside himself with grief. He closed his eyes and told Lakshmana to untie the bundle and examine the jewels.

Lakshmana did so and said, "There is no doubt these are Sitha's jewels! Often have I seen them while putting my head at her feet in reverence! The others I am not familiar with, never having examined them closely."

Rama's grief was unbearable! Seeing Sitha's belongings were bittersweet! He had not seen or heard from Sitha directly or indirectly for too long, and it was adding fuel to the fire of his grief. He had not kept his wife safe.

"Even a stranger, when he sees a helpless woman taunted or ill-treated, will give his life to save her, but I have failed my own wife who followed me into the wilderness and trusted me implicitly. I have failed her miserably."

Sugreeva's heart went out to Rama in his suffering. He knew what it was like to lose a kingdom and a wife. He and Hanuman spoke words of encouragement. They elaborated on a plan to save Sitha and bring her back. Eventually, the discussion became a council of war, and they planned on how to set forth and search without rest until they found Sitha. Hanuman spoke practically at this point.

He said, "First thing is to vanquish Vali. Then Sugreeva should be firmly reinstated as ruler. After that, we can assemble our army. To find the great Rakshasa, Ravenna's current residence, is not a small feat! We need a large army to explore every nook and cranny at the same time and rescue the noble lady from her captors. Therefore, the first action is to deal with Vali. Let's go!"

They went through forests and mountains until finally reaching the Kiskinda Mountain.

Rama said to Sugreeva, "You go ahead alone and call out Vali for a fight. I will hide while you fight, and at the appropriate moment, I will shoot my arrow and kill him."

Sugreeva now trusted Rama entirely.

He ventured forth alone and shouted, "Vali! Vali! Come out and meet me now in a battle—if you dare! If you face me in combat, I will kill you!"

These words resounded through the forest and reached the ears of the sleeping Vali, who, at the thought of his brother challenging him, sat up and chuckled.

He said, "Yes, yes, here I come!"

Tara, his wife, interceded, begging, "Please do not go out now. There must be an extraordinary reason your brother is behaving in this manner."

Vali shouted, "Get out of my way, my wife. Sugreeva is desperate, lonely, and going crazy. That's all. Nothing is as serious as you fear. I will be back in a moment with the blood of my brother."

Tara said, "He must have some powerful support, or else he would not dare behave in this manner. Be careful!"

"Dear wife, do you forget that whoever opposes me gives me half his strength? How can anyone escape me? It is only someone senseless that would lend support to my brother."

Tara quietly said, "Some persons who are interested in our welfare told me of a rumor that Rama has moved into these parts and lends Sugreeva his assistance. Rama has an invincible bow and has given new hope to Sugreeva."

"Oh, foolish one, you are betraying a gossipy tongue. I know about Rama—more than you do. He is one possessed of integrity and a sense of justice—one who would never do the wrong thing. He gave his kingdom to one brother and held all his brothers very dear in this world! Would such a person take sides in a quarrel between brothers? Are you aware that he denounced his right to the throne and took a life in the forest so that he could help his father fulfill an ancient promise? How can you slander him? Even if the entire world opposed him, he needs no power other than his great bow, Kodanda. Would he expect a miserable monkey like Sugreeva to help him find his wife? Rama who has gifted away his birthright to his younger brother—would he take sides in a family quarrel among strangers? Stay, beloved! I will be back in the twinkling of an eye!"

Seeing the mighty figure of Vali appear on the mountainside, Rama whispered to Lakshmana, "Have you ever seen such a dominant figure? Including all the gods and the demons?"

Lakshmana had fears. "I am not certain whether Sugreeva is trying to involve you in anything other than a battle between these monkeys. I am not comfortable as to whether we should participate in this struggle at all. How can you trust an ally who does not hesitate to plan to kill his brother?"

"Why limit it to monkeys? Strife between brothers is common, even among humans. Brothers like Bharatha are rare. Don't get too analytical about a friend."

During this discussion, Vali and Sugreeva clashed. They drew blood from each other. The air filled with their roars and shouts. Fire flames burst out of their enraged eyes and engulfed the surroundings, burning the mountains and frightening the gods who came to watch the fight. They danced around in combat and rolled on the ground. They tried to grab and strangle each other. It was impossible to judge who was winning. Finally, Sugreeva was beaten, punched and mauled so badly that he withdrew, baffled and paralyzed.

He found a pause, approached Rama, and gasped, "Help me, I can't bear it anymore ..."

Rama said, "While you are grappling together, I cannot easily differentiate you from Vali. Why don't you take that flower garland from that tree and wear it so that I don't kill you by mistake?"

With renewed hope, Sugreeva tore a garland growing on a tree and wore it. He screamed and fell on Vali with a thunderous shout. Vali laughed derisively and hit him in his vitals. Sugreeva was sure the end had come and cast a pleading look toward Rama. Vali lifted Sugreeva over his head, preparing to dash him to the rocks to kill him. Rama took the arrow from his quiver, aimed at Vali, and let it go. The arrow pierced Vali's chest. Amazed, Vali paused for a moment and with one hand held on to the arrow's shaft, arresting its passage through his chest. He held with such determination that even Yama, the god of death, nodded his head in appreciation. Vali laughed derisively at his own cocksureness and with all his strength pulled the arrow from his chest. He bowed his head in respect for the unknown assailant. Blood gushed from his wound, and at the sight of it, the grief-stricken Sugreeva wept.

In wonderment, Vali took the arrow and read the name Rama on the shaft.

"Rama? Instead of being in your abode and doing good deeds, why did you go out and, abandoning the breeding and your ancestry, stoop to this? How could you do this? You have destroyed the qualities and honor passed down through generations in your family! Is it the separation from your wife that has made you lose all sense of fairness and act recklessly? If Ravana acted treacherously, does it justify you coming here to kill the head of the monkey clan, unconnected with this affair? Has your breeding taught you only this? What evil have I done that you should destroy me thus? Who will wear the badge of honor in this world if you have thrown it away so lightly? You have killed me as an assassin—hiding behind a tree. You prevent others from doing wrong, but does that justify your erroneous actions? It is a grievous sin for a royal prince to kill an innocent person in this manner! Do you now have the right to be angry at Ravana for his wrongdoings? How false and undeserved is your reputation for honesty, truth, and tolerance! When strong men commit crimes, they become heroic deeds. My greatest sorrow is that a sinful wretch kills me. If you did this to recover your Sitha, I would have gotten her back for you in a day. I would have plucked Ravana from his palace, and flung him at your feet. No matter where he had hidden Sitha, I would have found her and brought her back to you. All those born must die; this is the law! I do not grieve for my death. Still, your sin is great for killing me in this treacherous way!"

Rama softly came from his hiding and approached the dying Vali.

"When you pursued Mayavi to the cave, your brother waited as promised for a very long time. In his anxiety, he started to follow your path into the tunnel, since he feared you might need help. His army chiefs and councilors in your court held him back. They pressed him to rule as a trustee for the time being. When you came back, before he could express his joy at seeing you alive, you beat him in the presence of others and attempted to take his life. Even after you realized he committed no wrong, you abused your power and left him alone only because you could not go to Mount Matanga—mere self-preservation. Even now, you would have squeezed out his life but for my arrow. You violated his wife's honor and made her your own. Guarding a woman's honor is the first duty laid on any rational being. You abuse your power and your limitless strength, and you act dishonorably because no one can judge you. You know the laws of conduct and morality, and yet you abused your brother's life partner instead of affording her protection. Sugreeva asked for my friendship and help, and I felt it was my duty to assist him."

Vali replied, "You are making an error based on your standards—not by our standards but human standards. My brother may be my enemy, but I feel it is my duty to protect and help his wife in his absence. I could not leave her unprotected. You make too much of my taking my brother's wife. The sanctity of marriage and the relationship of men and women in wedlock are for humans and are not known to us. Brahma has decreed for us absolute freedom in our sexual pursuits, habits, and lifestyles. We have no such thing as wedlock. We are not a human society. According to our society, I have not committed any sins. Please keep that in mind."

"I am not misled by your appearance or your explanation. Indra, the chief of gods, begets you. You are wise enough to know right from wrong. Creatures in human shape may be called animals if they demonstrate no knowledge of right and wrong, and conversely so-called animals that display wisdom and integrity cease to be animals and have to be judged by higher standards. Your strength, given to you through your steadfast meditation and prayer to Shiva, is superior to even the five elements. One who is capable of such achievements is judged by the highest standards of conduct."

"I'll accept what you say, but instead of standing in front of me and killing me, why did you aim your shaft like a hunter from a hiding place?"

Lakshmana gave the answer, "Rama had promised to support your brother Sugreeva when he came seeking help. If he had come before you, you might have made a similar appeal, which would have caused confusion. He did not want to break his promise, and that's why he shot unseen by you."

Realization dawned, and Vali felt that what he had done was wrong.

He said, "Now I realize Rama acted righteously. Forgive my rudeness and thank you for honoring me by treating me as an elevated being and not as a mere monkey by birth. You have made me understand and bestowed on me a vision of god. I have only one request. I hope my brother proves worthy of your trust in him. Treat him kindly. Sugreeva only engineered my salvation. I do not have the opportunity to catch Ravana for you, but Hanuman will obey you in all matters and capture Ravana at your command. Let him serve you!"

Then he turned to Sugreeva. "Don't sorrow for my death. He who has struck me is god himself, and I feel privileged! Please serve him well."

He turned to Rama and handed Sugreeva over to Rama as his choice for succession.

"My son, Angada, will be fatherless. You and Sugreeva should look after him. I entrust him to you. Look after him, and don't let him pine away. Ask him to treat Angada as he would a prince. Let Sugreeva know that Tara did not set me up against him. Do this for me! The warriors in heaven are calling."

The powerful Vali's life left its earthly cage and ebbed away.

Later, Vali's wife, Tara, and his son, Angada came down from the hillside carrying Vali's body. Their lamentations were heartrending.

Rama ordered the arrangements for Sugreeva's coronation and for Angada to be the second in command. With elaborate rituals, Sugreeva was crowned.

He approached Rama with deep gratitude and said, "I am ready to serve you, sir. What is your command?"

Rama put his arms around his shoulders and embraced him.

"Go back to your palace and govern. Gather around you those that have integrity, courage, and sense. Whatever you do, conduct yourself within the accepted lines of conduct. Even when dealing with enemies—and you treat them sternly— do not offend with words; always speak sweetly. Even in jest, do not hurt with words, not even the lowliest being," he said, remembering how he had made fun of Kooni's deformity when he was young and pelted her with clay balls with a catapult. He thought that possibly Kooni bore a grudge against him and got back at him by instigating Kaikeyi when Dasaratha was ready to make him king.

"Do not think of taking other peoples possessions."

He described how far one should surrender one's judgment to another—especially out of love.

"Not too far," he said, referring to his own pursuit of the golden deer in order to satisfy Sitha.

"Women can cause the death of men. You can see that from what happened to Vali. You have learned that from my experience. Uphold all that is honorable. Elders will tell you that this is the way of kings. Go and come after the monsoons are over."

Sugreeva pleaded, "Do me the honor of returning with us as our guest in the palace. Except that it is where monkeys live, it is more luxurious than the home of gods. Until the right time and the weather is such that we could search for Sitha, please come live with us."

Rama said, "Not now. If I live in the palace, I will not be fulfilling the vow I took to living in the forest for fourteen years. If you have me as a guest, all your attention will be on me. You will not be able to devote your attention to the obligations of ruling your kingdom. After the rainy season, come with an army and help me look for my wife."

Hanuman said, "I have no existence now, separated from you. I will serve you! I will be with you forever!"

Rama replied, "Go back with Sugreeva to Kiskinda and help him. He will need your support and judgment in carrying out his duties. The responsibility he has inherited is immense, and your first duty will be to help him. Come to me after four months—after the rains—and I will tell you what you can do for me."

After seeing Sugreeva and Hanuman off, Rama and Lakshmana went to reside on a hill. Lakshmana again constructed an ashram where they could spend the rainy season.

Anger and Reconciliation

The rainy season had begun. Dark, thick clouds rolled in, and the forest grew darker. The birds became quiet, and animals sought shelter from the expected storm. For a fleeting moment, lightning lit up the forest. Claps of thunder followed, and then everything was still. Suddenly, sheets of rain came down. The monsoon rains began with a vengeance!

Sugreeva and his retinue spent the time in Kiskinda in enjoyment, but Rama and Lakshmana spent the days waiting in a cave nearby for the rains to cease. All through the months, the rains poured, thunder rumbled, and lightning streaked the sky. Forest paths flooded, and the waters carried down boulders. Strong winds shook the trees, and foliage and dust scattered in the air. The monsoons were here. All life seemed paralyzed. Rama was depressed.

Lakshmana noticed Rama's state of mind and tried to comfort him.

"Please don't lose heart. Hanuman will soon be here. Angada and an army will be here to help us. Soon the skies will clear, and you will have Sitha by your side. Don't let your spirits droop."

Such words comforted Rama, and it helped him through the second bout of rain.

The rains ended at last. The skies cleared, and the animals stirred. New leaves appeared on the trees, and fragrant flowers bloomed. Rama's spirits lifted! Now he could get out of the ashram and act positively toward finding Sitha. With the change of season, Rama wondered why Sugreeva and his army had not come.

He said to Lakshmana, "Does it not seem that Sugreeva exceeded the four months? With our help, he has acquired a large kingdom to rule, but he has forgotten us. One who betrays a friendship needs to die! But first will you find out what has happened and why he has defaulted? Does he deserve to be punished? Tell Sugreeva destroying evil is within the code of conduct. Tell him if he does not help search for Sitha as promised, we will not hesitate to kill every monkey in this world so that the tribe will become extinct. If he found supporters other than Rama or Lakshmana, we are ready to meet any challenge from anywhere."

With this angry tirade, Rama felt he may have gone too far, and Lakshmana might act violently, so he said, "Speak gently. Don't show your anger, but make your statements firmly and clearly. If he has an explanation, be patient, listen carefully, and bring me his reply."

Lakshmana, properly armed, went immediately. He avoided the familiar paths taken to Kiskinda and moved swiftly along a different route. He was uncertain of his welcome and unsure of his relationship with Sugreeva, and he took precautions to avoid Sugreeva's spies. He reached Kiskinda, and the observers at the outskirts went and reported Lakshmana's arrival to Angada.

Angada hastened to welcome Lakshmana, but after detecting Lakshmana's angry demeanor from a distance, he rushed to Sugreeva's palace to inform him of Lakshmana's arrival.

He found Sugreeva in a drunken stupor, surrounded by beautiful, well-perfumed women. Sugreeva lay still.

Angada softly approached his uncle, saluted respectfully, and whispered, "Listen to me, please. Rama's brother Lakshmana has arrived and looks angry. What is your command to me now?"

There was no response from Sugreeva.

Angada left in search of Hanuman and took him to meet his mother, Tara. He explained to his mother what had happened.

Tara lost her temper and cried, "You have all indulged in immoral deeds without any thought to morality or the consequences resulting from your actions! After you get what you want, you forget your responsibilities! You are ungrateful. Though I repeatedly told you that it was time to help Rama, you never listened! Now you must face the consequences of your indifference and inaction! You don't realize the hardships Rama is undergoing. How difficult it is for him to stay alive.

You are self-indulgent, with no thought for others—selfish and ungrateful! You ask now what you should do! If you plan to wage war against Rama, you will be destroyed. What is there for me to advise you?"

Word spread quickly, and when the citizens heard, they locked and barricaded their doors. Lakshmana watched with amusement and irritation, and then, with a kick and push, shattered the blockade and flung the gates open. The monkey population fled into the nearby forests, deserting the city. Lakshmana stepped in and looked about the city.

Angada and the others stood surrounding Tara and said, "What shall we do now?"

Hanuman counseled Tara, "Please move to the threshold of the palace with your attendants. Lakshmana will not go past you. Otherwise, I dread to think what will happen if he rushes into the palace."

"All of you leave now," Tara said, "and remain out of sight. I will go and face him."

By the time Lakshmana had traversed the royal palace grounds and reached the palace, he heard the jingle of anklets and bangles. Looking up, he saw an army of women approaching him with determination. They surrounded him, and he felt embarrassed. He bowed his head, unable to face anyone, and stood with downcast eyes wondering what to do. Tara addressed him with courtesy.

"We are honored and overjoyed by your visit, but your coming has frightened us. Until we know what is on your mind, we will feel uneasy. Is there anything you wish to tell us?"

Lakshmana looked up and said, "My brother wants me to find out why Sugreeva has not kept his promise to bring an army to help us."

Tara truthfully replied, "Don't be angry with Sugreeva. He has not forgotten. He has sent out messages to all his associates—everywhere—in order to form an army, and he is awaiting their responses. This is the cause of the delay. Please be patient! We know that Rama's single arrow is enough to vanquish all enemies, and our help is only nominal."

Lakshmana looked relieved.

Noticing the change, Hanuman approached him, and Lakshmana said, "Did you, too, forget your promise?"

Hanuman said, "Rama is always on my mind. I cannot forget him."

He spoke with such humility and sincerity that Lakshmana's anger finally left him.

Lakshmana said, "Rama's pain is deep. He needs Sugreeva's help and fears that the longer he delays, the stronger the enemy may grow."

Hanuman replied, "Please step into the hall. Forget the past and come in."

Accepting Hanuman's invitation, Lakshmana followed Hanuman into the palace. After receiving him, Angada immediately went in to announce his arrival to Sugreeva. Tara withdrew with her companions. Angada explained to Sugreeva that Lakshmana was there and had arrived in a foul temper. He told him how the gates of the city fell at his touch.

Sugreeva said, "Why didn't anyone inform me of Lakshmana's arrival?"

Angada gracefully avoided a direct charge and replied, "I came in several times and spoke to you, and I thought you were awake, but you were asleep."

Embarrassed, Sugreeva said, "You are very considerate to explain it this way, but I was drunk, and it made me forget my responsibilities and promises. Wine saps away one's energy, senses, judgment, and memory. One cannot even distinguish between mother and wife, and promises are forgotten. Already born in a state of self-delusion, the wine adds further delusions. There is no salvation for us. We turn a deaf ear to the advice of wise men and the lessons they point out! We forget the good done to us by friends and the evil done to us by enemies; instead we skim the insects off the fermented froth, down the drink, and sink into oblivion! How can I face Lakshmana now? I vow in the name of all that I hold sacred I will not touch alcohol again!"

After this resolution, he felt braced up.

"I will now receive Lakshmana. Welcome him with the best hospitality and have public celebrations in his honor."

Angada got busy with the necessary preparations. When Sugreeva and his entourage went to meet Lakshmana, it was festive and cheerful, with music, flowers, and incense.

Sugreeva looked majestic and extended his hand in welcome to Lakshmana.

Lakshmana suppressed the tinge of anger that he felt at the first sight of Sugreeva, clasped his outstretched hand, and they entered the palace hall.

When Sugreeva invited Lakshmana to sit on a golden seat, Lakshmana said, "Rama sits on the ground; I don't need anything more than that," and he sat on the floor. The ministers and all those who witnessed this stood up!

Saddened, Sugreeva asked, "Would you like to have a bath and partake of our meal?"

Lakshmana said, "Rama in his grief does not eat! Every minute I delay here, he will be going without food. I need to go and find roots and greens for us to eat! Start a search for Sitha immediately, and that will be equivalent to a bath in the holy waters of the Ganges and offering me a meal of ambrosia."

Ashamed, Sugreeva said, "When Rama is suffering, only a monkey like me thinks of physical enjoyment. Forgive me."

Addressing Hanuman, he said, "We have not heard from our friends yet. Send the soldiers returning with the messengers to Rama's ashram! I will go now!"

He gathered his troops and followers and solemnly proceeded to meet Rama. He felt guilty about his previous conduct.

Rama met him with open arms and said, "Sugreeva, how is your kingship? Are your subjects happy and well?"

Sugreeva, filled with remorse, said, "I have failed in my duty to fulfill my promise, and I lost myself in self-indulgence!

I have betrayed the limits of the monkey behavior! Though I do not deserve it, please forgive me."

"The rainy season was long, and I knew you must be waiting for it to end. You now appear determined to support us, and this makes me happy. Where is Hanuman?"

"He will come presently with an army."

"Is that so? That is good news indeed! It is late now. Why don't you go back, attend to your duties, and come back tomorrow with your armies?"

"I'll do that. We can plan our campaign at that time."

So saying, Sugreeva and his entourage left. Lakshmana then reported all that happened in Kiskinda to Rama.

The Search for Sitha

Meanwhile, vast numbers of soldiers were assembling under the command of their leaders. They came from distant forests, mountains, and coasts. The sky darkened with the dust kicked up by the foot soldiers. Sugreeva showed the soldiers their campsites and went up the hill to show Rama the vast army assembled in the valley.

Rama's hopes revived as he watched the army, and he said, "Let's not delay. Let them start the search for Sitha."

Sugreeva divided the army into eight divisions and sent them in all eight directions to find Sitha. Hanuman and Angada were to precede south, the most important direction. Sugreeva gave detailed instruction to Hanuman on the route to take and the important landmarks he was to pass.

"I will give you thirty days. After that, I want you to return and report to me."

Angada was just leaving when Rama said, "How would you recognize Sitha?"

He then took Hanuman aside and started giving him an exact description of Sitha's appearance.

After describing Sitha to Hanuman, Rama said, "When you have seen this person, and she is alone, approach her and talk to her. Ask her whether she remembers what she said when she saw me from the balcony for the first time. She told me later that after seeing me from the balcony, she told her handmaidens that if anyone other than the one she saw from the balcony snapped the bow, she would kill herself."

Rama removed his signet ring from his finger and gave it to Hanuman, saying, "Give this ring to Sitha! She will then know that you are a messenger from me. Dear Hanuman, may you find Sitha and bring us together again."

Hanuman and Angada started southward with a handpicked army. They traveled across rivers and over mountains. Wherever there was a possibility that Ravana may be hiding, they searched every nook and cranny for Sitha.

The armies that went north, west, and east returned after a month and reported that they had not found Sitha. Rama, satisfied that they had done their best, was hopeful that Hanuman was having better luck.

Hanuman and Angada went far south, leaving no stone unturned in their search for Sitha. After wandering into a cave from which they could not find their way out easily, they lost valuable time, and a period had passed. They found themselves on the mountaintop overlooking the coast.

The soldiers, filled with blank despair, spoke among themselves and said, "We so confidently said we could find Sitha. How can we go back to Rama? There is nothing more for us to do. We have failed. We have exceeded the time limit. We can't face Sugreeva. Should we renounce the world and become ascetics, or should we take poison and die?"

Angada cried, "If we return to Kiskinda without a clue as to the whereabouts of Sitha, the king will punish us with death. He hates me! If not for Rama, he would never have made me second in command. Instead of going back and losing our lives, let us fast here and seek death now."

Hanuman said, "What talk is this? Sugreeva is a good king whom we need not fear. Let us return and beg for Sugreeva's forgiveness."

Angada said, "I do not agree with Hanuman. Sugreeva has no love or pity for me. He is cruel and does not want me to live and be his heir. I don't know what to do!"

He spread the *kusa* grass in the customary way to prepare for the vow of death, bowed to the gods and the dead, and facing east and determined to die, sat in the posture of a fast unto death. The soldiers cried in grief and followed suit.

One of the leaders of the party, a wise bear named Jambavan, was a devotee of Rama and said to Angada, "There is no one in your bloodline for the throne other than Sugreeva and you. You are your mother's only hope and heir apparent for the throne. It is your duty to live. You must go back and tell Rama the truth. He will perhaps tell you what to do next. Tell him the others have ended their lives."

Hanuman said, "Do not despair or give up! There is still much for us to do. If we are to die, let us die in battle. Remember Jatayu? How he died nobly? Fighting Ravana to the last?"

From a neighboring hill, Sampati, the vulture king, saw what was happening. He had lost his wings and, unable to move, was starving to death. He was heartened by the thought of many dead monkeys providing him with food. When he heard Jatayu's name mentioned, he perked up. Jatayu was his brother. After hearing of his death, he wanted to find out what had happened.

When they were young, Sampati flew with Jatayu. Jatayu flew too close to the sun and was about to burn up, but Sampati spread his wings over his brother and protected him from the sun. As a result, Sampati's wings burned off, but Jatayu was safe. Unable to fly, he fell down on a hill and since then had stayed in the same place. He was barely alive and was always hungry.

"Who brings sad news of my brother, Jatayu? Is beloved Jatayu dead indeed? Why did Rama go to the forest? Why did Ravana kill Jatayu? Tell me all," he cried in agony to Hanuman and his warriors.

They got up and led him gently down the hill.

Then they exchanged information, and Sampati said, "It has been a life of great suffering for me, and I survived while waiting for my redemption to come—hearing the name of Rama uttered within my earshot."

In unison, Hanuman and his men shouted, "Victory to Rama!"

On hearing this, the eagle went through a transformation; his feathers grew, and he shone with fresh beauty. He found solace in performing the funeral rights for his brother, Jatayu.

Sampati's eyes had not lost their keenness, though he was old. When he found that Hanuman and his warriors were in despair about finding Sitha, he said, "Ravana went this way with Sitha. I saw him carrying Sitha off to Lanka. Sitha is captive in Lanka, surrounded by Rakshasas. You will have to cross the sea. Do not be alarmed by the expanse of water before you; you will succeed."

He described in detail the wealth of Ravana's kingdom.

He then took their leave and went, saying, "In Jatayu's absence, I have to take on his duties. Our tribe has been without a leader for too long."

After he had left, they discussed how they would cross the sea. Anxiety and fear overwhelmed them. Jambavan spoke once again.

He said to Hanuman, "You are the only one who can cross the sea! Not fire, nor water, nor wind can destroy you! You have powers granted you by the gods. Being the son of the wind god, you are equal to him in intelligence and power. For all your strength, you are virtuous and modest. You can expand yourself to cover the world in one stride if you so wish. Make yourself as immense as you wish, and with one foot here, put your other foot on the shores of Lanka. When you reach Lanka, make yourself as small as you can, and your devotion to Rama will lead you to where Sitha is captive."

Hanuman listened, and, reminded of his might by Jambavan, Hanuman's form began to change. His stature assumed a gigantic size. The soldiers were amazed and filled with wonder and joy.

"This hill, Mahindra Hill, can stand my weight. I shall see Sitha and shall bring you good news."

He stood there, looking southward, and choosing his own moment, he stepped across to Lanka.

Hanuman Meets Sitha

Landing on the shores of Lanka, Hanuman shrank himself to the size of a little monkey and went in search of Sitha. He peeped into every building he came across, and many housed Ravana's women from all parts of the world. In one particular house that was ornately furnished, he saw a beautiful woman reclining while many attendants fanned her. He looked closely at her features, thinking that this could be Sitha, and mentally compared her to the description given by Rama.

He was disgusted with himself for thinking that the woman in the palace, sleeping carelessly in a stranger's chamber, covered with jewels, was Sitha. The woman he was looking at was Mandodari, Ravana's wife. He moved on and finally saw Ravana in his palace. After satisfying himself that Sitha was not in the palace, he decided to search the woods and the gardens.

In his search of the parks, he came across Asoka Vana, a magnificent park with orchards and gardens—Ravana's favorite retreat! Swarms of bees were hovering around the fragrant blossoms. Lotus flowers were blooming as they drifted in the ponds nestled among the rocks. Swans were preening their feathers as they floated, and colorful birds were singing as they flitted around the orchard, eating the ripe fruits. Dragonflies were avoiding the frogs by the water, and large trees provided shade.

Hanuman climbed a tree and saw below fierce-looking, armed Rakshasa women sleeping—with Sitha seated in their midst. He watched her closely and was overjoyed. He had no doubt that he had found Sitha! She looked dusty and unkempt, with a single yellow sari covering her. The Rakshasa women woke up and began tormenting her with threatening words uttered close to her face. She shrank back from them but challenged them to do their worst.

On seeing Ravana approaching, the Rakshasas drew back from Sitha. Ravana addressed Sitha with endearing words. Well hidden in a tree covered with foliage, Hanuman saw everything that went on below. Sitha shook with grief and fear.

Ravana said, "Oh beautiful one! Why do you shrink from me? It is lawful for a Rakshasa to take another man's wife, but I plead for your love. I shall never touch you until your heart belongs to me. You have nothing to fear. My one wish is that you should care for me as I care for you. My wealth, my kingdom, Lanka, even the whole earth will be yours to enjoy! You will rule all the queens and women in the palace. I long to see you decked in jewels and fine clothes. Even in your present state, you have drawn me away from my other wives. You have captivated my heart. Why do you waste your thoughts on wretched Rama?

In what sense can Rama equal me? Do you not see that I am superior to Rama in every way? Have pity on me. Only say yes!"

Sitha placed a blade of grass between them and, laughing derisively, said, "Ravana, perish these inappropriate thoughts! It is wrong for you to desire me. Turn your heart to your wives. Never can I agree to what you ask. I cannot be your wife. I am married. Do not bring sorrow on yourself by continuing this foolish desire."

Spurned by Sitha, Ravana went off in a rage after ordering the fierce women to break her will. Sitha trembled as the women menacingly surrounded her again.

Piteously, she cried, "Rama, have you forgotten me?"

After a while, the women retired. Hanuman watched as Sitha got up and started gathering hanging tree roots and making a rope. After a while, she began testing the rope she had made and attempted to throw it over a sturdy branch. Concluding that she was trying to hang herself, from his hiding place behind the branches, Hanuman decided to recite the story and virtues of Rama softly so that only Sitha could hear him. In a sweet and gentle voice, he began to sing the story of Rama.

He concluded, "Grief-stricken Rama went in search of Sitha. He met and befriended Sugreeva, who helped him by sending his troops to search the whole world. These soldiers could assume any shape they wished. They went in search of Sitha all over the world. Following a clue given by Sampati, I crossed the sea and came here. I see you are exactly as Rama described as his spouse."

She looked around in all directions and saw only a sweet monkey seated on a branch above her. Hanuman, radiant with joy at having found Sitha, descended, palms together, and bent his head in salutation.

He said, "May I know who you are? Are you the Princess Sitha carried off by Ravana?"

"Indeed I am Sitha, daughter of the king of Videha, and Rama's wife. For twelve years, I enjoyed happiness in Ayodhya. In the thirteenth year, King Dasaratha prepared to crown my husband. Then Kaikeyi, his youngest wife, demanded the boons he had promised her. The first was that Dasaratha crown Bharatha, and the second that Rama live as a hermit in the forest for fourteen years. I went with Rama and Lakshmana to the forest. Ravana carried me off and has kept me prisoner here in Asoka Vana. He has given me twelve months to accept him as my husband, and if not, he will kill me. I have two months of the twelve left. When they are over, I shall end my life."

Hanuman asked, "Can you tell me what you told your handmaidens when you saw Rama from your balcony the first time?"

Sitha replied, "I told them if Rama was not the man who successfully bent the bow and married me, I would kill myself."

Convinced it was Sitha, Hanuman comforted her and quickly told her who he was and why he was there. He showed her Rama's ring. Sitha had saved a single piece of jewelry knotted at the end of her sari.

Sitha, sure that Rama sent Hanuman, gave Hanuman the jewelry and said, "Go fast, my lord! You will soon meet my husband. Be safe. Tell him of this incident that even Lakshmana does not know. He will know that I told you of this. One day, god Indra's son came as a crow and scratched my chest with his claw when attempting to get at my breast in lust. Angrily, Rama took a grass blade and sent it flying toward the crow as an arrow. The crow fled in terror and approached the gods in heaven. They told him to go back and fall at Rama's feet and beg his forgiveness. When he came back, Rama forgave him but said that henceforth all crows would have sight in only one eye. The gods, seeing this, showered Rama with garlands of flowers. Go now. You came and gave me hope to live longer."
Hanuman assumed an enormous stature and left Sitha and headed north. He decided to let the Rakshasas know the might of Rama's army by doing one great deed. He destroyed Asoka Vana, hoping that the Rakshasas would come to investigate. He would kill as many of them as he could. Ravana would follow in anger, and he would cut off his ten heads and go back to Rama.

Hanuman immediately put his plan into action. He trampled large trees and disturbed the birds that rose up and squawked in fright. He saw the sleeping Rakshasas who were guarding Sitha wake up, look around at the destruction, and flee.

Hanuman made so much noise that he was sure Ravana would hear it and send his army to capture him. Hanuman saw the army of large Rakshasas with fangs and mighty shoulders approach gleefully. They bared their teeth, pounded their shoulders, and came in a pack, kicking up a dust storm. Hanuman was happy everything was going according to plan.

As they approached, shooting and throwing weapons at him, he rose to his full height, uprooted a large tree, scooped up the army in one hand, and hit them with the tree with the other. Blood poured from them, and they fell in a mangle to the ground and died. Eventually, he managed to kill the whole army.

After some time, Hanuman saw a large army of Rakshasas on elephants charging toward him. The mighty Hanuman was not at all tired and looked forward to meeting the new foe. He banged the clouds together in great thunder that shook the earth with great drops of rain and blinded the Rakshasas with lightning. The venomous snakes came out of caves spitting their poison and scared the Rakshasas. The earth and mountains split. He saw the elephants lose control and the riders fall to the ground.

They arranged themselves again and started the battle by releasing their weapons at Hanuman. Hanuman caught the weapons effortlessly and broke them. He picked up an iron rod and sprang down from the entrance to Asoka Vana. He twirled the rod in the midst of the army and destroyed the elephant, chariot, horse, and infantry.

Later, Hanuman saw another battalion approaching, led by royalty. First he thought it was Ravana at a distance, but then he knew it was not Indrajit but another son of Ravana—the younger Aksha Kumar.

As Aksha Kumar approached, he sent a hail of arrows directed at Hanuman, who swatted them away with the iron rod he held in his hand. As Aksha Kumar increased the strength and numbers of arrows he sent, Hanuman jumped on the roof of the prince's chariot and grabbed at his bow. They fought for possession of the bow, and Aksha Kumar drew his sword and tried hacking at Hanuman. Hanuman took the bow and broke it and threw it away. Wrapping his tail around Aksha Kumar, Hanuman sat on him and bashed his head with both hands, killing him. His lifeless body rolled in a bath of blood. Seeing, this the Rakshasas who came with Aksha Kumar fled, some taking the form of birds and flying away while others jumped into the river as fish. Some lay next to the dead bodies and pretended to be dead.

Looking toward the palace Hanuman saw an angry Indrajit riding his chariot hard and approaching him. As Indrajit prepared for battle, Hanuman uprooted a large tree.

All Indrajit's arrows fared the same fate as those sent by his brother. Indrajit took the bow he had won in a battle with god Indra and with it shot hundreds of arrows at a time. Hanuman, wounded all over, used the tree to remove the arrow shafts from his body. He then hit Indrajit with the tree on his jeweled head and caused him to bleed profusely. Indrajit was stunned but recovered and continued shooting arrows at him. Angered by this, Hanuman carried Indrajit and his chariot and flung it to the ends of the earth. The chariot came crashing back to earth. Indrajit, realizing that nothing worked on Hanuman, finally decided to use the king among weapons, the Brahmasthra. Recognizing the mighty weapon that had taken the form of a giant snake and wrapped around him, Hanuman allowed himself to fall at the entrance to Asoka Vana. He decided to keep his eyes closed in respect of the weapon sacred to Brahma.

He heard Indrajit approach with some of the Rakshasas. They were shouting delightedly and creating a commotion.

They shouted, "Kill this monkey with your arrow! Cut him with your sword!"

Hanuman wanted to meet Ravana and speak to him, so he allowed Indrajit to bind him and drag him along the street to Ravana's court. He wanted to present the truth to Ravana in the presence of his ministers and elders so that he would be aware of Rama's power to command his army to destroy Lanka. Maybe Ravana would allow him to take Sitha back to Rama.

Indrajit stopped with Hanuman at the palace entrance and sent word to Ravana. He then obeyed his father and took Hanuman to his court.

Hanuman raised his head in Ravana's presence and looked at him. He thought, *Maybe I should shrug off the Brahmasthra from my shoulder and kill Ravana now, take Sitha, and return to Rama. Is it right for me to kill Ravana and not let Rama do it? That would not be right. Only Rama should be able to kill him. It is impossible for anyone else to do so. If I start a war with him now, it would only cause a delay. Sitha would kill herself. I will just act as a messenger.*

Indrajit said, "Your Highness! Here stands a warrior in the form of a monkey but with the courage and strength of Lord Shiva and Lord Vishnu."

Ravana, hearing his son's words, angrily asked Hanuman, "Who are you? Why did you come here? Are you Lord Vishnu? Are you Indra? Are you Lord Shiva? Are you Lord Brahma? Are you a demon sent to destroy all of Lanka? Which of these are you? Who sent you? In order that I should know you, answer me correctly!"

Hanuman replied, "Ravana! I am none of those. I am also not one who is here to represent one who is weaker than I. I came to Lanka as a messenger to a mighty warrior. If you wish to know who sent me, I will tell you in detail. Listen carefully.

"He is here because of all the sages, gods, creatures, and those that are harmed by your strength, riches, and the powers awarded you by the gods that you abuse. He incarnated as the son of King Dasaratha who ruled the earth. He is one that the Vedas and dharma proclaim as the one true god. Wisdom, compassion, and boons bestowed by honest penance are all on his side. He came down to help the gods who have been tormented by you. My name is Hanuman, and I am just a messenger sent by Angada, the son of Vali. Sugreeva sent his army to look for Sitha in all directions, and I am with the southern army. I came here alone and found the princess and spoke to her. I came here to give you the message that King Sugreeva wishes me to deliver. It is just! It behooves you to listen to what I say and understand.

"You have not followed dharma, and you will ruin your life if you continue. You have lusted after another man's wife and have taken her from him. That is a grievous fault, and your destruction is imminent. It is not too late. You have lost the purity you gained through your penance by losing control over your desires. By tormenting one so chaste and pure as Princess Sitha, you have lost your honor, and what little pride you have will be gone after tomorrow. Sin cannot conquer virtue. If you want to regain your honor, your life, and your wealth, return Sitha to Rama now! This is the message that King Sugreeva wished me to deliver to you."

Ravana laughed mockingly and said, "Very well said! This is said to me, one who is so well versed, by a monkey living on a hill! Leaving that aside, why did you kill my Rakshasas?"

Hanuman replied, "I did not have anyone to take me to you, and so I destroyed Asoka Vana. Without asking me why I did this, the Rakshasas attacked me. I only killed those Rakshasas who tried to harm me. After that, I came here peacefully to deliver this message to you in person."

Ravana was furious and said, "Kill this monkey!"

Ravana's brother, Vibishana, stood up and said to those preparing to kill Hanuman, "Stop!"

He approached his brother and said, "Oh learned one! You who rule the three worlds, could you kill a messenger? There might be women killers in some worlds, but nowhere is a messenger ever killed. If you do this, it will destroy our honor and pride. You will give the gods reason to jeer at us. Rama had

Lakshmana cut off Soorpanakha's nose to send you a message. If you kill this messenger, who will be able to tell Rama and Lakshmana about our might?"

Ravana, still angry, said, "Brother, you give good advice. Let us send him back to describe our power."

Addressing Hanuman, Ravana said, "Go describe what you saw and bring Rama and Lakshmana back soon."

To his men, he ordered, "Wrap his tail with rags soaked in oil, set it on fire, and take him around the city for all to see. When you are done, take him to the boundary and send him on his way!"

Indrajit ordered the men to remove Brahmasthra and replace the serpent with rope to tie around Hanuman. After they did this, they dragged Hanuman through the city streets. They stopped at the city limits and tied rags around his tail, doused it with fuel, and set it on fire.

Hanuman, happy that he did not have to disrespect Brahmasthra, shook off the ropes and the men and ran over the rooftops, landing on buildings and setting fire to them with his tail.

After destroying most of the capital and making sure the tree under which Sitha sat was safe, he rushed off to report everything to Rama.

Ravana Plans Retribution

The Rakshasa king, Ravana, was afraid and ashamed at what Hanuman had done to Lanka.

He summoned his ministers and said, "What happened is strange and unexpected! This messenger from Rama not only entered Lanka but he met and talked to the imprisoned Sitha. He then destroyed our temples and palaces, and people are afraid now. Rama has become an enemy. We must come up with a course of action to take. Let's not forget that my authority is challenged not by a warrior, but by a monkey! What were our chiefs and armies doing? We do not even have the satisfaction of saying we caught and killed the monkey! What do we do next? I want you all to feel free to speak your mind."

Ravana's commander in chief said, "Envying a man and taking Sitha from her husband is not the work of a hero. Rama and Lakshmana have wiped out warriors such as Kara and fourteen thousand troops. You have not killed Rama and Lakshmana. We must go forth and hunt and kill those that inspired the monkey. We must act. Now is not the time to dwell on the past!"

After many ministers spoke praising the king, his brother, Kumbhakarna, rose up, quieted the ministers, and said, "Brother! You hold me in high esteem as your younger brother, and I will share these heartfelt words with you."

"Go ahead!"

"King of Lanka! There was no one to match you in this clan for putting Brahma first. Now you are thinking of the destruction of your kingdom. You have carried out a morally unacceptable deed! You desired and abducted another man's wife, which is against all codes of ethics. You ignored her cries and appeals. Is this the right thing to do? You have kept her imprisoned all these months and brought on us this present catastrophe. You are ashamed of the destruction of our city. You have disgraced your wives and repeatedly fall at the feet of another man's wife and worship her! Though she repulses you, you ignore her words and consider her your love. Is this praiseworthy? Abducting her was the day of the Rakshasas downfall! Do you want to return her to her husband and seek peace? If we do, it will bring disgrace to us. It is better to die in battle trying to keep her! Think carefully! Since we have gone this far, let us fight for her possession. I am ready to lead an army against our enemies."

After listening to Kumbhakarna, Ravana was pleased and said with affection, "Brother! You have said it well! I too came to the same conclusion. Let's kill all our enemies and return! Let us go to war today!"

One after another, the ministers and warriors got up and spoke words to please Ravana. Then all of them stood up and, raising their weapons, roared aloud.

Vibishana, Ravana's younger brother, made them all sit down, and said, "Brother, what these people say is sweet to hear but not right or upon which to act. If you take their advice, it will mean the destruction of Lanka. It was not right! It was a great sin for you to have seized and brought Rama's wife here! What harm did Rama do to us? What Rama did in the Dandaka Forest to protect those who looked to him for protection was self-defense. He killed only those who went to kill him! It does not justify your action of abducting his wife! When a fault is yours, it is morally incorrect to think of war. My advice is let us restore Sitha to Rama and ask his pardon before Rama and his army attack Lanka. This way we can save our kingdom, lives, honor, and possessions. Dear brother! Don't be angry with me! I only say this for your good."

Ravana's son, Indrajit, lost his patience and burst out, "My uncle's words fill me with shame. What race are we? What is our strength? My uncle has only betrayed his evil intentions. Are we afraid of two petty humans? Did I not beat Indra and his multitude of gods in a battle? Vibishana's advice is an insult to our race!"

Vibishana said gently to Indrajit, "My boy, you lack experience. That is why you are talking this way. My lord! Please listen to me. Do not reject what I say! The only way is to return Sitha honorably to Rama and ask his forgiveness. Failing to pursue this will only result in our destruction."

Ravana pummeled a fist into the palm of the other hand repeatedly. He laughed sneeringly through all his ten mouths. All his eyes spurted fire, and sparks flew.

He shouted, "I have had enough! If you were not my brother, you would be dead by now! You are a disgrace to our race!"

Unable to bear further insults, Vibishana said, "My brother, I thought that I could serve you in your time of need, but you won't let me. God bless you. I am going! May god bless you!"

Renouncing all his possessions, Vibishana rose in the sky and proceeded to Rama's camp with four of his good friends.

Hanuman Returns

The sight of Hanuman returning brought joy to the assembled warriors.

Jambavan welcomed him with great affection and said, "We are eager to hear a full account of your journey."

Hanuman recounted all that happened in proper sequence and said, "Our efforts have been successful because Sitha has been chastity incarnate. The Rakshasas should have burnt to ashes when they carried her away."

Sugreeva, Rama, and Lakshmana heard of the arrival of Hanuman and of the rejoicing of the warriors and waited impatiently for their arrival. Leading the soldiers, Hanuman and Angada entered the palace.

Hanuman said, "I have seen the goddess of purity, your queen. She is safe and well in Lanka."

Sugreeva and Lakshmana, beside themselves with joy, embraced Rama.

"Dear Hanuman! Tell me—where is Sitha? How is she? Where is she? Tell me all!" said Rama.

Hanuman told the whole story to the eager listeners.

Rama wept when Hanuman repeated the words of Sitha, "Rama has slain many Rakshasas, but why has he not come as yet to kill Ravana? Why has he not sent brave Lakshmana to kill the wretch? My lord is not indifferent to me, is he? I have not committed any sin in thought, word, or deed to lose his love."

Hanuman said, "I tried to console her by saying, 'Rama grieves for you and knows no rest. Rama and Lakshmana have not forgotten you. They will come with Sugreeva and his warriors to destroy Ravana and return with you.'

"She gave me a treasure and said, 'Friend Hanuman, give this to Rama. Convey the news of my welfare to the lions and to King Sugreeva.' She said she would struggle and stay alive for a month, but then she would either be killed by Ravana or take her own life."

Hanuman, following Sitha's instructions, gave her jewelry to Rama.

At the sight of the jewel, Rama was overcome with grief and joy and said, "Oh, Lakshmana!"

He embraced Hanuman and said, "Heroic son of Vayu! You have indeed brought her to me!"

Vibishana Meets Rama

Rama stood at the edge of the sea deep in thought. His goal was so close now; he was sure that he would triumph over Ravana.

While he was brooding, he heard some commotion nearby, followed by an unfamiliar voice crying loudly, "Oh, Rama! I am here to ask for asylum. I seek your protection."

Rama dispatched an envoy to find out what was going on. The emissary reported back to Rama that it was Vibishana seeking asylum after leaving his brother. Rama consulted his companions on their view of the visitor.

Sugreeva said, "You cannot trust one who is disloyal to his brother who treated him with love and affection! My brother was no friend of mine, and he did not treat me kindly. We cannot admit him into our camp. You are on a mission to kill all Rakshasas, and for all his noble speech, this person is a Rakshasa."

Jambavan came forward to say, "We take a risk when we allow anyone from the enemy camp into ours, and it will be too late when we discover his trickeries and disguises. Remember, what happened to be a golden deer turned out to be Mareecha."

Rama listened to everyone. The majority opinion was to reject Vibishana's plea.

Rama looked at Hanuman and said, "Hanuman! You are quiet. What are your thoughts?"

Hanuman said, "I hesitate, but since you ask me directly, let me assure you that this man is not evil. If someone approaches you to seek refuge, regardless of who they are, in your position, you should help them. I do not agree with the others that he is bad. He has come because he heard of your help to Sugreeva, he heard you surrendered your kingdom to Bharatha, and he admires and adores you! He is sure you can help him. He tried so hard to save his brother but failed. In Lanka, I peeped in his home and found that, unlike the rest of his family, his home is sparse and reflects the home of a man of purity and godliness. When Ravana ordered me killed, Vibishana persuaded him to spare my life, saying I was only a messenger. At that time, he did not intend to leave Lanka. He is genuine and asks for your help. We should take him without further thought."

After listening to Hanuman, Rama said, "I agree with you. We should give asylum to one who seeks our protection. It is our first duty to protect. Even in defeat because I trusted him, I would not mind it because I would have done the right thing. If I refused him, even in victory I would feel empty. Go to him—tell him we accept him! Welcome him and bring him here."

Soon, Sugreeva brought Vibishana to Rama. Vibishana's eyes filled with tears of joy at meeting Rama. He fell at Rama's feet and worshipped him. Rama bent down and held him with both hands, and lifting him up, he embraced him.

Rama said, "Until the end of eternity, I will give you today the wealth of Lanka! First we became five brothers with Guha. Then Sugreeva made it six, and you will make it seven brothers."

A humble Vibishana accepted Rama's friendship.

Finally, Rama turned to Lakshmana and commanded, "Treat him as the ruler of Lanka—now in exile. Honor him as a king and make him comfortable!"

Vibishana said, "It is not my intent to take the crown of Lanka, but since you confer it on me, I accept. Believe me, the only reason I came here is to be with you and receive your grace."

They met daily and discussed the weapons Ravana had and the strength and placement of his troops, thus enabling Rama to plan a more precise attack of Lanka. Rama's biggest worry was how he and his army would cross the sea to Lanka. Rama prayed and fasted for seven days and asked the sea god to help him pass.

The sea god said, "Rama, earth, air, ether, water, fire these five elements must follow the eternal laws of their nature. I am as much subject to the laws of nature as the other elements. What can I do?"

Rama got angry and threatened to shoot his arrows into the sea so that the water might evaporate and allow him to go.

The sea god pleaded, "Don't destroy the sea creatures. Ask your people to bring trees and boulders, and I will accept and use whatever it takes to bridge the sea."

He then showed Rama the best site to build a causeway. Sugreeva sent for Nala, the royal architect of the monkeys, and ordered him to start work on the bridge at once. Sugreeva asked Jambavan to rally the troops to help Nala.

Jambavan said in a booming voice, "Everyone except Lord Rama, Lord Lakshmana, King Sugreeva, and Lord Vibishana can start working on building the bridge under Nala's command!"

Rama's men, thousands of Vanaras (monkey warriors), bears, and elephants brought in huge rocks, pieces of mountains, and pebbles and piled them to create a causeway. Nala took everything they brought him and arranged it painstakingly to build a long, wide bridge.

After three days, the bridge was completed, and Vibishana, Sugreeva, and others went to give the good news to Rama. Rama went to see the bridge and praised Nala lovingly and thanked him.

Rama and all his armies used this passage to march across and reach Lanka.

BOOK 3

Rama

At War

Battle in Lanka

In preparation for the impending battle with Rama, Ravana deployed his trusted generals and relatives to protect the key approaches to the capital. Rama distributed his army to meet Ravana's challenge, and the army rested on a hill for the night.

The following morning, standing on the summit, Rama and his army took a good look at Lanka. Observing the great and beautiful buildings in Lanka, Rama felt sorry.

He said, "Because one person has committed a sin, all this wealth and the whole Rakshasa race is destroyed. What a pity that this son of a noble race should forget his real greatness and bring death and destruction on himself and his people!"

Rama's army descended from the hill and entered the forest adjoining the city of Lanka. His army surrounded Lanka in the way he had planned.

Ravana sent one of his men to corrupt Sugreeva, who was one of Rama's staunchest supporters. He attempted to mislead Sugreeva, but it did not work. When he returned and reported to Ravana that a causeway had been built and a large force was getting ready to cross over, Ravana sent two of his ministers, disguised as monkeys, to scout the enemy camp.

As Vibishana inspected his Vanaras in preparation for battle, his vigilant eyes dwelt on two of the Vanaras who did not appear to fit in. He pulled them out and punched them. As they lay senseless, he bound them with rope and pulled the bleeding villains to present them to Rama.

Seeing them, Rama said to Vibishana, "Even if they have wronged us, can we torture them? That is bad. Don't torment them. Please release them."

Vibishana replied, "My lord! These are not Vanaras; they are Vanaras only in appearance. They are spies sent by Ravana! They are two Rakshasas named Sukhan and Chaaranan."

The two tried to talk their way out of the situation by saying that they were really Vanaras and that Vibishana had an ulterior motive in wanting more power and planned to eventually kill Rama. Vibishana got angry and recited a mantra, and instantly the two spies appeared in their true forms as Rakshasas.

Seeing their faces, Rama could not help chuckling and said, "Do not fear! Tell me why you came here."

They answered, "We came on orders from Ravana, taking the form of Vanaras to escape detection, to observe and report back to Ravana."

Rama said, "We have given the kingdom of Lanka to Ravana's brother, Vibishana. We along with our armies have crossed over and come to Lanka. It was only because we did not know where Lanka was and how to get here that Ravana was spared all these days. Even if he has Siva guarding him, we are going to destroy Ravana, the one without dharma, the one who killed our father, Jatayu. The evil one who imprisoned Sitha will burn in hell. Make sure you convey all this to him and leave."

Shouting, "We are free! We are alive!" they fled!

Ravana's heard the message that the spies brought back. He went to the turret of his castle where he had a perfect vantage point to see across to the hilltop where Rama was camped. He saw Rama on the peak of the mountain.

Rama, looking over at the beautiful city of Lanka, saw Ravana and his entourage on the turret.

He said, "Vibishana, can you see the people on the turret? Will you please identify them for me?"

Before Vibishana finished identifying Ravana, Sugreeva, with sparks flying from his eyes, bound over to the turret and seized Ravana.

The Rakshasas heard the thunder of Sugreeva landing on the turret and rushed off in all directions, leaving behind Ravana. Sugreeva stared intently at Ravana, standing in front of him like a mountain.

In an angry voice, Ravana demanded, "Why have you come here?"

Sugreeva punched him, and Ravana, astounded, started hitting him with all twenty hands. He managed to bring him to the ground and started grinding him with his feet on the limestone floor. Sugreeva caught his feet and wrestled him to the floor, and Ravana's cavernous mouths started spouting blood. When Ravana recovered and Sugreeva realized he could not quell the demon, he grabbed Ravana's crown gems as a trophy and went back to Rama.

Rama stood, sadly wondering if Sugreeva had finished the job that he, Rama, had set out to do. While he stood worrying, suddenly Sugreeva appeared before him and dropped the crown jewels that he had taken. Rama hugged him and washed his wounds with his tears.

Rama said, "My dear friend Sugreeva! If anything had happened to you, even if I beat Ravana, wouldn't I have been the loser? We should not give in to anger but should couple valor with patience. It was rash of you to rush off and attack Ravana without consulting anyone. You are a king and have to act more responsibly."

Sugreeva looked down said, "Protector of all, Sri Rama, I am sorry. I shamelessly thought that I could beat your arrow and bring Ravana's ten heads back to you. Instead I am lucky to have come back alive, yet I brought back the jewels on Ravana's crown."

Vibishana said, "That is something only Lord Shiva could have done. You did well, my friend."

Rama praised Sugreeva and said, "I would consider it a victory because you took his jewels from his head and came back."

Ravana, ashamed that the gods had witnessed Sugreeva taking his crown jewels, retired directly to bed. He was not tempted to spend time being entertained by the ladies of the court. At dawn, his scout arrived and reported to him on the activities and positions of his enemies. Ravana called a council meeting.

The ministers said, "The monkeys have surrounded us, and fighting has started. Please tell us what you would like us to do."

One of the generals jeeringly said, "Monkeys blocking our city's entrances! The gods themselves left their armaments and ran when you fought them. What can these unarmed monkeys do?"

In response, another minister said, "It is not too late to stop this by returning Sitha to Rama. A monkey crept into this city and set fire to it! Did Hanuman have a spear? An arrow? Any arms? What about the unarmed monkey Sugreeva who ran away with all your crown jewels? Before we are subjected to Prince Rama's arrows, let us attain peace and prevent any more destruction. Is there another choice?"

Ravana got up in anger and shouted, "You have lost your status in my court because of your cowardice! Therefore, you do not have the right to speak."

With this, Ravana sent his generals in the planned directions, with Indrajit going to meet against Hanumans army.

Rama went to the northern gate to await the arrival of Ravana.

He looked at Vibishana and said, "Vibishana, I have an idea that I have researched. Let us send a messenger to Ravana and tell him that if he returns Sitha now, your life will be spared. If he refuses, it is right that we begin the battle against him. This is the right thing to do."

Vibishana replied, "I agree with you."

Sugreeva also agreed, but Lakshmana said, "Showing mercy to enemies repeatedly is wrong. He is the one who caused the gods so much harm. We should declare war."

"Brother, I know someone other than Hanuman who can go as messenger and hold his own. I would like Angada to warn Ravana to prepare for death and to come and meet me in battle, or return Sitha to me"

When Angada delivered this message, Ravana told his Rakshasas to seize and kill him. Angada rose to his regular, giant size and, shaking off the two Rakshasas, kicked and broke off the tower of the king's palace. As soon as Angada returned, Rama gave his army the order to begin attacking Lanka.

The war started in earnest. The Vanaras destroyed the arrows that were destroying the mountains that they hurled at the Rakshasas. Some of the boulders met their mark, and Rakshasas fell to the ground with their heads split. The Rakshasas arrows killed many Vanaras. Sugreeva fought valiantly and jumped on the general's chariot. He pulled the general out and stomped on him and killed him.

On the other side, the Vanaras were being hurt by the Rakshasas. Neelan, the son of the god of fire, got angry when seeing this and hurled a huge tree at the Rakshasas. This disrupted the ranks of Rakshasas who were on chariots, and the horses, elephants, lions and *yalis* fled in different directions, leaving the army in disarray. The Rakshasas turned away from the front lines and fled.

At one of the other gates, arrows that were launched from a great distance were beating the Vanaras. Seeing this, the chief of the bears, Jambavan, dug up a huge mountain and, snarling, stood in front of the marksman and threw the mountain at him. The chariot, horses, and the charioteer were destroyed. The marksman faced Jambavan, and they fought. Ultimately, Jambavan was victorious. The Rakshasas returned to the city defeated.

Ravana's world began to shrink. As the battle raged, he lost his associates one by one.

He even tried to trick Sitha by ordering a sorcerer to create a head resembling Rama's head. He placed it in front of Sitha as evidence of Rama's defeat. Though shocked at first, Sitha regained her composure.

The fury of the battle grew. Neither side could distinguish night from day. The battle noises of jeers and cheers, challenges and death throes were heard. Buildings were destroyed, and trees uprooted. The monkeys were swarming Lanka. The giant monkeys fought valiantly and courageously with logs and stones against Ravana's well-armed soldiers.

Indrajit attacked Rama and Lakshmana with darts made of living serpents. When the snakes attacked Rama and Lakshmana, they fainted on the field. Indrajit rushed back and told his father, Ravana, that he had killed Rama and Lakshmana and would vanquish the leaderless army soon.

Ravana rejoiced and said, "Go tell Sitha that Rama and his brother are no more. Take her high up in my chariot Pushpak Vamana and show her their dead bodies on the battlefield."

Sitha was happy to hear that she would be able to have a glimpse of her loved ones and accepted the chance. When she saw her husband's inert figure, she broke down sobbing.

One of Ravana's Rakshasa women whispered to her, "Don't believe it, they are not dead ..." and she explained why they had fainted.

In due time, Garuda, the mighty eagle and the natural enemy of all serpents, swooped down and scattered the venomous snakes away. With the effect of the serpent darts removed, the brothers were on their feet again.

When Ravana heard the cheers of the enemy, he was surprised. He sent his commander in chief, his son Indrajit, and a few others he could rely on, one by one. He felt shattered when the news came of the death of his commander in chief.

Ravana said, "No time to sit back! I will go myself and destroy Rama and his horde of monkeys." He got in his chariot, entered the battlefield, and found Lakshmana obstructing his path to Rama.

At this encounter with Ravana and his chariot, Lakshmana fell down unconscious.

Hanuman hoisted Rama on his shoulders so that he could be level with Ravana and his chariot and charged Ravana. Finally, the principal combatants met, resulting in Ravana being sorely wounded with a broken chariot. Barehanded, he stood before Rama—helplessly!

Rama said, "Go now and come back tomorrow with fresh weapons."

Ravana had to accept a concession. He dejectedly went back to his palace.

Entering his palace Ravana ordered Kumbhakarna, his brother, to be woken up from his deep sleep. Kumbhakarna was the only one Ravana could depend on to fight Rama. After placing large quantities of food close to him, they woke him up with difficulty. Kumbhakarna was disoriented, and his hunger was phenomenal!

When he had eaten and drunk his fill, Ravana's chief minister said, "My lord, the battle is going badly for us."

"Which battle?" Kumbhakarna asked, not awake fully.

"Your brother has fought and is losing to his enemies. They are breaking in; our fort walls are crumbling ..."

Kumbhakarna jolting into consciousness, said, "Why didn't someone tell me this before? I will deal with Rama! It's not too late!"

Kumbhakarna had never seen Ravana so dejected.

He went into Ravana's chamber and said, "My brother! Is it as I predicted? Is your reputation on earth and in the heavens ruined? Has the time arrived for the demolition of the Rakshasas? It is impossible to defeat Rama! You still have Sitha imprisoned. Release her to Rama and beg his forgiveness!"

Angrily, Ravana said, "You must be saying these things due to fright! You have lost your mightiness. You cannot fight anymore. You have been eating enormous amounts of meat and drinking a large amount of toddy! Now all you can do is to go to your palace and sleep day and night! Go! Get away from here!"

Ravana prepared for battle and then called for his chariot.

Seeing these preparations, Kumbhakarna fell at Ravana's feet and said, "Forgive me, my brother! You have gone on without heeding anyone's advice and brought this on yourself. Now is not the time to speak of dead events. I will stand by you. I will go to fight! I will not say that I will come back victorious. I feel fate is in the way; it feels as though it has me by the neck and is pushing me. If I die and don't return, you will realize that releasing Sitha is the best course! We will reap the benefits of doing that."

Rama saw in the distance the huge soldier coming toward them and said, "Who is that soldier?"

Vibishana replied, "That is Ravana's brother, Kumbhakarna. Killing him would be of no avail."

Rama said, "I agree. Sugreeva, why don't you try talking to him? Instead of fighting, ask him to join us."

Vibishana said, "My lord! Let me meet with him and speak to him."

Rama said, "Go and convince him."

When Vibishana arrived at his camp, Kumbhakarna was delighted. Vibishana worshipped at his older brother's feet, and brotherly love caused tears to pour from Kumbhakarna's eyes.

After listening to what his younger brother had to say, Kumbhakarna said, "I am happy that you joined Rama because at least you will survive. I don't know why he let you come alone to meet the enemy. Brother! Ravana nurtured and brought me up for a long time. Now in his time of need, he trusts me to go to war. I cannot allow my promise to be as written on water; I will not betray him. You will be the ruler of this world. Go soon and be with Rama, who is great! My death will bring me honor. Don't grieve when you think of us!"

Vibishana sadly returned to Rama.

The massive Kumbhakarna joined the skirmish and created havoc. Rallied by Angada, the frightened monkeys hurled rocks and dealt heavy blows with uprooted trees. Kumbhakarna smiled and ignored their efforts. His appetite was insatiable. He slew and swallowed hundreds of monkey soldiers, as he was more than a match in size to the monkeys. He was very close to finishing Sugreeva himself.

Rama went into the battle to give Sugreeva a hand. He sent the sharpest of his arrows toward Kumbhakarna. Though the arrows tore Kumbhakarna limb from limb, he continued to fight valiantly with only inches of his body remaining intact. Rama sent another arrow and severed Kumbhakarna's head.

The loyal and gallant Kumbhakarna fell dead, fighting his brother's battle.

When Ravana heard Kumbhakarna was dead, he was heartbroken and cried, "My right hand is cut off!"

One of his sons said, "Why should you despair? You have Brahma's gift of invincibility. You should not grieve."

Another son, Indrajit, said, "Knowing Rama and Lakshmana's might, why have you not sent me? If I am here just to carry a sword and be a weight on earth, I am not your son!"

Indrajit gathered all the special armaments given him previously by gods and set forth. His chariot with a thousand lions to pull it and which could beat Shiva's chariot was waiting for him. He created a figure resembling Sitha, took it before Rama's army in his chariot, and slaughtered it for all to see.

The monkey soldiers, believing it to be Sitha, were demoralized and cried, "What is the point in fighting when our goddess Sitha is gone?"

They were despondent until Vibishana came and rallied them again.

He said, "I know my brother well! Never will Ravana allow Sitha to be killed. He wants her too much! He is tricking you!

Indrajit has gone to perform a sacrifice, and, if completed, he will be all-powerful, and we will not be able to kill him. Lakshmana should go and stop him!"

Lakshmana, accompanied by Hanuman and other warriors, went to the spot where Indrajit was preparing to perform his sacrifice to the evil spirits. Lakshmana thwarted the sacrifice, and a fierce battle ensued. Indrajit ascended his chariot and sent forth arrows. Standing on Hanuman's shoulders, Lakshmana did the same. He destroyed Indrajit's chariot, and the combat continued on the ground.

Finally, Lakshmana uttered Rama's name and discharged the fatal arrow. Indrajit's severed head fell and shone like fire. The gods showered flowers from the heavens. Lakshmana, wounded and bleeding, slowly went to Rama, assisted by Hanuman and Jambavan. Rama rejoiced and showered Lakshmana with praise and love.

When Ravana heard of Indrajit's death, and of his brother Vibishana's hand in it, his grief and anger swelled.

"My son, the great warrior, vanquisher of Indra, you have left your mother, Mandodari, your wife, and me sorrowful! I have nothing to live for but revenge!"

He then sent his army to kill with a vengeance.

Rama's arrows killed most of the army, and Ravana prepared himself for battle. He dressed for war and came out of his palace. He ordered his biggest chariot drawn by a thousand horses. He stood in the chariot and invoked his favorite god,

Siva. He held his bow in his left hand. He then took all the armaments he needed for war. He had his necklaces on his neck over the armor. His heroic appearance was breathtaking. With his mighty warriors by his side, he drove out to battle.

The gods in heaven saw Ravana riding out to battle flying his flag, surrounded by his soldiers, elephants, chariots, and horses. Not wishing Rama to be at a disadvantage, the gods asked Indra to send down his special chariot for Rama's use. When the chariot appeared at his camp, Rama was impressed. He wondered how it had appeared in his camp.

"Sir," the charioteer said, "my name is Matali! I am the charioteer for Indra. The gods, Brahma and Shiva, have commanded me to bring this chariot here for your use. It can fly fast—over mountains, sea, or sky or any obstacle—and will help you defeat Ravana in battle."

After Rama consulted with Lakshmana and Hanuman, and being convinced that this was not a Rakshasa trick, he climbed into the chariot and began the battle.

Ravana had ordered his charioteer to speed ahead, but Rama said to his charioteer, "Ravana is in a rage and is running around aimlessly. He is bound to exhaust himself. Until then, we don't have to hurry forward. Move slowly. I will tell you when to go faster. At that time, follow my instructions closely and promptly."

Ravana's soldiers were killed one by one, and he found himself facing Lakshmana. Forcing himself past Lakshmana, he ended up facing Rama. He sent a barrage of arrows at Rama, who stopped these arrows with his own. Rama turned and looked at the army supporting Ravana. The Vanaras had slaughtered a large number of them. The Rakshasas guts were scattered all over the battlefield, and heads rolled. They even crippled the horses drawing their chariots. Rivulets of blood flowed. Rama thought that the destruction of his soldiers might be a way to save Ravana, but it only spurred him on.

Rama's army made way for Ravana's chariot, unable to face the force in its pathway. Ravana blew his conch in shrill challenge, and of its own accord, Mahavishnu's conch sounded in answer to the challenge. Matali picked up Indra's conch and blew it, signaling the beginning of the actual battle.

Ravana sent a spate of arrows toward Rama. The flags on the chariots clashed, and the stringing and twanging of bowstrings on both sides overpowered all other sounds. A shower of arrows followed from Rama's bow.

Ravana gazed at the chariot sent by Indra and swore, "These gods, instead of supporting me, have chosen to support a mere human! I will teach them a lesson! I will capture Rama and his chariot, fling them to high heaven, and dash these gods to destruction!"

In spite of his oath to seize Rama, he dispatched another spate of arrows toward Rama, who rained arrow for arrow.

Ravana changed his tactics and went up higher. He started attacking the monkey army supporting Rama.

Rama ordered Matali, "Our young soldiers are being attacked from the air. Let's go up higher and follow Ravana."

There followed an aerial pursuit at dizzying speed across the sky. Ravana's arrows came down like rain, but Rama's arrows diverted, broke, or neutralized these arrows.

One of Ravana's arrows killed Matali and the horses. Rama paused in grief and then continued with his offensive.

The divine eagle Garuda returned and perched on Rama's flagpole on the chariot. The gods thought this was a good omen. The chariots continued their clash and circled the globe several times. The twang of the bows of the warriors sounded like the crashing of waves. Horses sped by, their hooves not touching the ground, and elephants charged as if they were in must and chasing after female elephants. As the battle continued over Lanka, one of Rama's arrows pierced Ravana's armor, and he winced.

The fight became one of attacks and parries with supernatural powers. When Ravana invoked these supernatural powers, a variety of arrows appeared. There were arrows spurting flames, arrows with bloody faces, arrows with a ghostly appearances, arrows that were like serpents, arrows with poisonous tips, and others that could swallow the sun and the moon, which resulted in darkness on one side and light on the other, cyclones on one side and rain, lightning, and thunder on other sides, and showers of rocks on another side.

Ravana invoked a power called *danda*, a special gift from Shiva. This was a weapon designed to find the target and destroy it. When Ravana aimed and sent it, the arrow spurted flames when it was airborne and went toward Rama. Rama launched an arrow and brought it down.

Next, Ravana invoked a weapon called *maya*, which created an illusion and confused the enemy. It created an illusion of reviving the army and leaders who had died—Indrajit, Kumbhakarna, and others—and bringing them back to the battlefield. Rama found those that he thought were dead coming on with battle cries and surrounding him.

Rama asked Matali, whom he had revived by now, "Is this an illusion? How are all these coming back? What is happening?"

Matali said, "In your original form, you are the creator of illusions in this universe. Ravana has created phantoms to confuse you. If you make up your mind, you can dispel them."

Rama immediately summoned a weapon called *gnana*, which means wisdom. When he sent it, all the armies that had appeared suddenly vanished. Rama was showered with flowers and garlands by delighted gods watching from the heavens.

Ravana then shot a weapon named *thama* that swallowed the sun and the moon, thus creating total darkness in all the worlds. It also created rain on one side, a rain of stones on another, a hailstorm showering down intermittently, and a tornado sweeping the land. Rama met it with a weapon named Shivasthra, which neutralized it.

Ravana used his deadliest weapon, a trident with extraordinary destructive powers gifted to him by the gods. It came flaming toward Rama, its speed and course unaffected by his arrows. Rama lost heart when he saw his arrows falling down without stopping the trident. As it came closer, he recited a mantra from the depth of his being. The trident collapsed. Ravana was astonished.

He wondered, *Is Rama a god? Not Shiva; Shiva is my supporter. Not Brahma; he is four faced. Not Vishnu, because I have immunity from the weapons of the trinity. Though he may be the highest god I will fight until I defeat and crush him or take him prisoner.*

Ravana next used a weapon that issued forth monstrous serpents with enormous fangs and red eyes, vomiting fire and venom. They darted from all directions. Rama selected a weapon called *garuda*, which meant eagle. Soon thousands of eagles got the serpents with their claws and beaks and killed them, maddening Ravana. He blindly emptied a quiver of arrows in Rama's direction. Rama's arrows met them halfway and reversed them so that their sharp points embedded themselves in Ravana's chest.

Ravana was weakening in spirit. Rama and Ravana were close enough to grapple with each other. Rama sent a crescent-shaped arrow, sliced off one of Ravana's heads, and threw the head far off into the sea. He continued this process, but for every head he cut off, another grew in its place. Rama cut off Ravana's arms, but they kept growing back. Ravana grew faint as more of Rama's arrows embedded themselves in his body. Ravana fainted!

Matali whispered, "Now is the time to finish him off. Go on."

Rama put away his bow and said, "To attack a man who is unconscious is unfair warfare. I will wait. Let him recover."

When Ravana recovered, he accused his charioteer, saying, "You have disgraced me! You withdrew. Those who watch will think I retreated."

The charioteer explained how Rama had suspended the fight. Ravana patted the charioteer on the back and carried on his attacks. Rama went on shooting his arrows to cut off all the miscellaneous items Ravana kept throwing at him. Rama paused.

After much thought, Rama decided to use *Brahmasthra*, a weapon designed by the creator Brahma so that Shiva could destroy an old monster. When all else failed, this weapon was used. Now Rama invoked it with special prayers and worship, and directed it in Ravana's direction, aiming at his heart rather than his head. Ravana had forgotten to add his heart when he prayed for indestructibility in his heads and his arms.

Ravana's oversight brought an end to his life.

Rama watched as Ravana fell to earth, his face aglow with a new quality. Rama's arrows had peeled off the crust of anger, conceit, cruelty, lust, and egotism from Ravana, and his real self—devout and capable of great attainment—showed. His face shone with serenity and peace.

From his chariot, Rama commanded Matali, "Set me down on the ground."

When the chariot came to rest, Rama said to Matali, "I am grateful for your services to me. Now you can take the chariot back to Indra!"

Rama, Lakshmana, Hanuman, and all his other war chiefs approached Ravana's body. Ravana's crown and jewelry lay scattered on the ground.

Rama said to Vibishana, "Honor him and cherish his memory so that his soul may go to heaven where he has his place. I will leave you to attend to his funeral arrangements."

Sitha's Return

After Ravana's death, Vibishana was crowned king of Lanka.

Rama said to Hanuman, "With the king's permission, go to Asoka Vana and tell her of all that transpired here.'

When Hanuman appeared and told her what had happened, Sitha was overjoyed. Hanuman wished to kill the Rakshasa women who were mean to Sitha, but Sitha would not let him, saying that they were only following Ravana's orders.

Vibishana arrived at Asoka Vana and humbly bowed at Sitha's feet.

He said, "My lady! The outcome we wished for has come to pass. Sri Rama wishes to see you. The gods have come to venerate you, and Rama wants me to bring you. Therefore, get dressed in the appropriate finery and prepare yourself to leave."

Sitha replied, "I will come as I am. It is not proper for me to get dressed and bedeck myself in jewels. The gods, my husband, and the people should see me as I am."

Vibishana said, "Mother, I am only saying this because Rama ordered me to."

"All right, I will do as he wishes," Sitha said, and went to dress.

The Rakshasa women hurried to Sitha and helped her dress. She was escorted to a chariot that took her to the final battlefield where Rama awaited her with a large crowd.

She was eager to meet her husband after months of loneliness and despair. She was disappointed that he did not meet her in private but accepted the situation. She prostrated herself at his feet and worshipped him. Rama decided to test her chastity.

Rama said, "My work is done! I have rescued you and fulfilled my mission! All this is to defend the honor of our race and to honor the values of our ancestors. After all that has happened, it is not customary to admit a woman back home after she has lived in the house of an outlaw Rakshasa under his rule. You dined in splendor there and enjoyed it. Even after your reputation was ruined, you did not die. After all this, how could you unashamedly come back? Did you think I would still desire you? I did not cross the sea and against all odds come to free you and destroy the arms-bearing Rakshasas to save you. I killed the Rakshasa because I did not want to be blamed for allowing another to steal my wife—you who have lost your love for me and relished and ate all meats and drank toddy in Lanka! Is this the type of meal you wished to prepare for us? You have lost your chastity and good behavior. You have lived like one born to a lower life. If a chaste woman had lived in sin, she would give up her life to be rid of that sin. What more can I say? Your evil ways are like a sword to my heart. There is only one thing you can do and that is to kill yourself. If not, you are free to go where you please and to choose any place to live. I do not want you to stand before me!"

Hearing Rama's fiery, harsh words the ministers, gods, women, Rakshasas, Vanaras, Jambavan, and his followers could not bear it and cried aloud.

Sitha was dumbfounded. She felt as though a burning brand had been inserted into an open wound. She looked up at Rama, and her eyes flashed fire.

She said, "My ears have heard the unworthy words you have spoken and broken my heart! Is this the reward I get for living blamelessly all these years? Are my trials not at an end as yet? I thought with your victory all our troubles were an end. You forget the family from which I come! Janaka is my father. Was it my fault that I was abducted, imprisoned by force? When Hanuman first met me, did he not describe to you my plight? It appears Hanuman is not a good messenger! I am a virtuous woman whose mind cannot be changed even by Brahma. If you who sees all cannot see this, what god can help me now? After you have wished for me to kill myself, there is but one course open to me! Fetch the firewood, Lakshmana, and light a fire!"

Lakshmana had been watching Rama's behavior in dismay and indignation. At Sitha's orders, he looked at Rama to see whether he would refute it, but to no avail. Obeying Sitha, Lakshmana, his eyes filled with tears, kindled a large fire.

Sitha circled the fire three times, saying, "Oh Agni, the great god of fire, you are my witness! You, at least, will know my purity and take me as your own or burn me unmercifully if there are any doubts."

The watching crowd begged Rama and said that this anger was unlike him. The goddesses covered their eyes, not wishing to witness this awful sight. The mighty gods shivered. The earth grew hot as Adishesha, the god of all serpents, withdrew his protection of the earth and spat out poison. The oceans dried up, lamenting loudly. Planets changed places.

Sitha bowed in prayer toward Rama and with palms folded jumped into the fire. The fire did not burn Sitha.

Agni rose from the heart of the fire bearing Sitha with all her clothes and jewels intact! The worlds righted themselves. The watching crowd danced with joy.

Agni said, "My lord, without consideration for my lowliness, you have destroyed my might with the pure fire of your wife's chastity. It appears as though your anger was directed to me too."

Rama said, "Who are you? You protected her from burning. Who instructed you to do that?"

Agni replied, "I am the god of fire. This maiden's virtue scorched me, and I found it unbearable. The judge of all beings, even after bearing witness to the pain I had to bear, would you doubt the purity of this maiden? The world was being destroyed when she jumped into the fire. At least now, accept her."

Saying this, Agni presented Sitha to Rama. Rama, satisfied that he had proved his wife's integrity to the world, welcomed Sitha back to his arms and whispered, "Did you think that I doubted your faithfulness even for a moment? I had to do this to satisfy the people. Without it, they would say that love blinded me, and I behaved with weakness."

The gods watched uneasily as Rama displayed the tribulations and limitations of humans. It was necessary to remind him of his divinity.

Brahma, the creator, came forward to address Rama and said, "Of the trinity, I am the creator. Shiva is the destroyer, and Vishnu is the protector. All three of us derive our existence from the Supreme Being—the Supreme God. We are subject to dissolution and rebirth, but the Supreme God who creates us is without a beginning or end! There is neither birth nor growth nor death for the Supreme God. He is the origin of everything, and in him everything assimilated in the end. That God is yourself, and Sitha, by your side now, is a part of the divinity! Please remember that, and let not human fragilities overcome you. You are all powerful, and we are blessed to be in your presence."

Rama Meets Dasaratha

In heaven, Shiva encouraged Dasaratha to go down to earth and meet Rama.

"Rama has carried out your commands and kept your promises. He has spent fourteen years to preserve your integrity and honor. You should meet him and bless him!"

Dasaratha descended in the midst of his family, in his human form. Rama was overjoyed to see him, and as was the custom, to honor his father he prostrated himself at his feet.

Dasaratha said, "For the first time in many years, my heart feels joy! Though I had shed my human form, the pain remained until this minute! I will now go back in peace, but before I go, ask me something, anything, I could do for you."

Rama replied, "Your arrival here is the greatest wish fulfilled, but if you insist, I would like you to make your peace with Kaikeyi and Bharatha. To me, they will always be mother and brother."

Dasaratha replied, "Bharatha is different! He has proved his greatness. I will accept him, but Kaikeyi is another matter. She ruined us all. I can never forgive her."

Rama said, "It was my mistake. I should not have accepted the kingship without considering the consequences. I should have paused to give it some thought."

Finally, as the king agreed, Rama felt a burden lifted from his shoulders. He felt at peace with the world. He bade farewell to his father. Dasaratha took leave of Sitha and Lakshmana and soared into his place in heaven.

Rama Returns to Ayodhya

When the time had come, the gods advised Rama, "Tomorrow you will be completing your fourteenth year of exile, and you must reappear in Ayodhya promptly. Bharatha waits in Nandigram for news of your return, and if you do not appear in Ayodhya, we dread to think what he will do to himself."

Rama, realizing the importance of his timely return, turned to Vibishana and asked, "Is there any means by which you can help me reach Ayodhya within a day?"

Vibishana replied, "I will give you the Pushpak Vamana. It belonged to Kubera, the god of wealth, before, but Ravana appropriated it for his own use. It will take you back as soon as you wish."

He then ordered his guards to bring the vehicle.

Rama, Sitha, Lakshmana, Sugreeva, Vibishana, and a whole army climbed into the magical chariot and travelled to Ayodhya. As the chariot flew, Rama pointed out various landmarks (including the causeway built to cross to Lanka) to Sitha. They stopped to visit a sage who had been hospitable to Rama once but sent Hanuman in advance to Nandigram to inform Bharatha of their arrival.

At Nandigram, Bharatha had been counting the hours for the end of the fourteenth year. There was no sign of Rama, and he was distraught. All his austerities and penances seemed fruitless. He had ruled as regent, with Rama's sandals on the throne, for fourteen years.

Bharatha summoned his brother Sathurugna and said, "I can't imagine what fate has befallen Rama, but my time is up! I pass my responsibilities to you. You will go back to Ayodhya and rule as regent."

He then ordered a pyre built and the fire lit. Sathurugna tried hard to dissuade him, but Bharatha was adamant that he would kill himself.

At this moment, Hanuman appeared in the form of a Brahmin youth. He quickly put out the fire.

Bharatha, taken aback, said, "Who are you? What right do you have to put out the fire I have started?"

Hanuman answered, "Rama sent me to inform you of his arrival. He will be here shortly." He then related all that had happened to Rama and Sitha in the fourteen years.

"Make an announcement and prepare a warm welcome with the people for the arrival of Rama and Sitha."

Bharatha immediately informed the city and prepared to receive Rama and restore him to the throne as king of Ayodhya.

Their mothers, including Kaikeyi, assembled at the village of Nandigram to receive him. When Rama's Vamana arrived, he greeted all those who had come to meet him with tears of joy. Rama fell at Vasishtha's feet and worshiped him. Vasishtha tenderly lifted him up and embraced him. Lakshmana did the same, and Vasishtha embraced him and kissed him on the forehead. The reunion was a happy one.

The brothers, Rama and Bharatha, met. Rama felt as though he was seeing his father when he saw Bharatha.

Tears of joy filled Bharatha's eyes, and carrying Rama's sandals aloft, he announced, "Your splendid brother Bharatha, who for fourteen years ruled this great kingdom without the desire to do so, and the enemy to the mother who bore him is here to see you!"

Bharatha prayed at Rama's feet, and joy from more than being king filled his being. It was a time of supreme satisfaction. His brother would ascend to the throne, Bharatha's vow finally fulfilled.

Rama, happy to see his mothers and all the people who had come to greet him, behaved like a calf that had been separated from his mother.

Sitha worshiped at the sages' and the queen mothers' feet. She received blessings from them all. Lakshmana also worshiped at the queen mothers' feet. They all spoke to him with love and praised him and blessed him.

Lakshmana, Bharatha, and Sathurugna hugged with great affection when Lakshmana worshiped at Bharatha's feet. Rama bade them all climb into the chariot, Pushpak Vamana, and the gods showered them with flowers as the chariot rose into the skies and hastened toward Ayodhya.

They stopped on the outskirts, and the brothers swam in the river. Rama discarded his austere garments, and he and Sitha adorned themselves as that befitting a king and queen.

With Bharatha driving, Lakshmana holding a parasol over Rama's head, and Sathurugna showering him with petals, they set off in a decorated carriage to the city of Ayodhya. On either side of the carriage, Vibishana and Sugreeva mounted on elephants and acted as guards. Angada rode in front of the carriage, with Hanuman bringing up the rear. The various armies, all in human form, mounted on elephants and followed. It was an impressive parade!

Sitha travelled in a carriage that resembled a chariot. An entourage of females in the guise of goddesses, riding on female elephants, horses, and palanquins, surrounded her. The gods and sages showered her with flowers.

Elephants, horses, and even the plants rejoiced when Rama finally arrived in Ayodhya. The citizens were overjoyed and celebrated in the streets. Rama and his entourage entered the palace, and Rama asked Bharatha to show Sugreeva and Vibishana around the palace. They were overwhelmed at the luxury and riches in the palace.

Sugreeva and Vibishana asked Bharatha whether they had set a time and date for Rama's coronation.

Bharatha answered, "When the sacred waters from the seven seas and the large holy rivers subside and come here, it will be an auspicious moment."

Sugreeva approached Hanuman. Hanuman crossed the globe and collected the holy waters from the seven seas and the holy rivers. Bharatha sent Sumanthra to fetch Sage Vasishtha. When the sage entered, everyone stood and offered him the golden throne to sit. They asked him an auspicious time for Rama's coronation. After researching, Sage Vasishtha fixed the hour for the coronation interrupted fourteen years before.

Rama entered Ayodhya after fourteen years of exile! The preparations, interrupted fourteen years ago, resumed! Rama's old friends and new friends were present. Hanuman, Sugreeva, and all the rest from Kiskinda were there in human form. Vibishana was an honored guest.

At the auspicious hour on the chosen day, Rama was crowned! He sat on the throne, with Sitha beside him and Lakshmana standing a step behind him. Hanuman knelt at his feet, looking up, with his palms pressed in worship.

With Rama as king and Sitha as queen, there followed a long reign of peace and happiness on this earth.

Epilogue

From various sources

Kamban's translation of Valmiki's *Ramayana* ends at this point in the story. Valmiki's tale continues until the death of all the essential characters.

After a time of peace and prosperity in Kosala, Sitha became pregnant and decided to visit the ashrams of the holy men dwelling along the Ganges River. Once, Rama casually asked his friends and his adviser what the universal consensus was about his brothers, his wife, and himself. With some reluctance, they disclosed that the citizens were critical of Rama for accepting his wife back, even though she had lived with Ravana in Lanka. They were worried that their wives would expect the same leniency from them that Sitha had received from Rama.

As a husband, Rama knew his lovely wife was blameless. As a ruler, he knew his subjects were unhappy.

He called Lakshmana aside and said, "Sitha is preparing to visit the sages and spend some time with them. Go with her!

Make sure she gets to the sacred stream, to Valmiki's hermitage, safely but return alone."

Rama retired to his private chamber and there gave way to his grief.

At dawn, Sitha, bearing gifts for the wives of the sages, set out in a chariot driven by Sumanthra, accompanied by loyal Lakshmana.

They reached the Ganges and Valmiki's ashram, where Lakshmana explained Rama's position to Valmiki.

When Sitha realized what was happening, she fell to the ground and cried. Lakshmana left her with a heavy heart as she lay sobbing and bereft.

Sitha took abode with Valmiki and his wife. Months later, she gave birth to twin boys, Kusa and Lava. They grew up with their mother and the holy hermits in the forest. Valmiki taught them wisdom. He also taught them the skill of reciting to music long poems. The twin boys chanted in perfect unison and learned to sing all the stanzas of the *Ramayana*.

A dozen years passed, and under Rama's rule, the country flourished. Rama decided to hold the Horse Sacrifice. It took a year to prepare, and he invited all the neighboring heads of states, holy hermits, princes, his subjects, Sugreeva, Vibishana, and their officers to the final ceremony.

As the time grew close, Valmiki came with his two disciples and stayed outside of Ayodhya. With the king's permission, Valmiki sent the children to the palace to chant the long epic, *The Ramayana*.

When the boys arrived in the palace, many remarked on their resemblance to Rama. They entered the crowded court and sang in sweet harmony, in praise of the king. They were pulling at Rama's heartstrings. The children seemed to know everything about his life. They captivated the audience.

Every night, the boys continued singing until the entire tale unfolded. At last, when the boys came to Sitha's abandonment, Rama knew these were his sons.

He sent word to Valmiki and said to the crowd, "I long to have Sitha by my side. I have never forgotten our love. If Valmiki could vouch for her loyalty in front of the assembly, and if she could prove her innocence to them, she could surely return to my side and share my throne?"

The people agreed wholeheartedly.

Sitha arrived in Ayodhya and entered the palace with Valmiki. Her eyes were downcast, and a tear trickled down her wan cheek.

Rama stepped forward, halted by Valmiki, who said, "Hear, oh King, Kusa and Lava are your twin sons! Sitha is pure and without fault!"

Rama said, "I declare to all that Kusa and Lava are my sons!"

He then looked at Sitha and said, "Faithful, devoted Sitha. I have never doubted your faithfulness! Forgive me for banishing you to please my subjects! It was shameful and wrong! I knew no other way to stifle the rumor."

The daughter of Mother Earth and a great king slowly said, "If Rama has always been foremost in my heart, and I have been loyal to dharma in my devotion and duty to my husband, then, Mother Earth, receive your child! Put an end to the pain and shame of my life and take me back!"

As she spoke, the earth trembled. The ground began to shake violently, and the rumbling got louder until, in a crescendo, it cracked with a loud noise. A golden throne, in the shape of a rosebud and supported by shimmering serpents, rose from the depths of the dark abyss. Mother Earth, peaceful and beautiful, sat on the throne with her arms outstretched toward her virtuous daughter.

"My child!" was all she said.

Sitha stepped into her mother's arms, her face aglow, and sat on the throne, supported by her mother.

As the crowds watched, astonished, the throne descended into the chasm, and the ground closed over it. Mother Earth and Sitha sank from sight, not leaving behind the smallest sign of the ground being disturbed. No one now doubted her innocence.

Rama was grief-stricken. He sent everyone home. He knew he would never see Sitha's human form again.

Seeing his grief, Brahma appeared and said, "Rama, do not grieve. Remember that you are the great Vishnu. You will reign with Sitha in heaven, once again, when she is your wife, Lakshmi. Valmiki's story will reveal your future!"

Years passed. Rama never took another woman as wife. He had a golden statue of Sitha built and kept it by his side. His kingdom prospered, but he lived a joyless life.

A few years later, queen mothers Kausalya and Kaikeyi died. Yama, the god of death, came from heaven and sought a secret conference with Rama. Lakshmana was left to guard the gate, with strict instructions that whoever interrupted the meeting should be killed. The celestial Rishi Durvasa came to see Rama and, when Lakshmana refused, threatened to destroy Rama's kingdom. Lakshmana decided that one death was better than multiple and sacrificed his life and let him enter.

Following Rama's orders honestly, Lakshmana went to the River Sarayu and surrendered his life by penances and went to heaven.

Rama's son Lava ruled in Sravasti, which was the capital of Oudh, at the time of the Buddha, in the fifth and sixth centuries before Christ. His other son, Kusa, founded Kusavati at the foot of the Vindhya Mountains.

Rama decided that it was time to leave his sorrowful, human life and resume his heavenly form as Vishnu. He informed his family. His brothers decided to join him and left their thrones to their children. Sugreeva, king of the monkeys, also joined him. Rama did not allow Hanuman to follow him.

He said to Hanuman, "Do you remember the wish that you asked me long ago? You said that you would live on earth as long as people spoke of my greatness. You will live here forever, and may you be happy."

Rama dressed in his silk fineries and, reciting ancient prayers, set forth to the banks of the Sarayu River. As he set forth on his final journey, the people of Ayodhya, monkeys, bears, and birds followed. Vibishana prepared the departure rites.

A serene smile lit Rama's face, and he shone radiantly as he stood by the riverbank. He told his brothers to follow his actions. He scooped water in his cupped palms three times and drank it. Then Rama submerged himself in the river and instantly rose again in the eternal form of Vishnu.

Rama and his brothers entered heaven in the form of Vishnu. All his followers, who had renounced their lives on earth, received their places in heaven. The gods smiled, rejoiced, and sent showers of flowers from the heavens.

Those who followed Rama assumed their godly forms and now live in heaven.

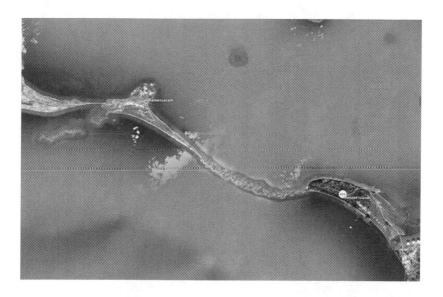

Adams Bridge to Lanka from Space Shuttle – NASA

Glossary

Asoka Vana: A beautiful park in Lanka where Sitha was imprisoned.

Ayodhya: The capital city of Kosala, modern-day Oudh, near modern-day Faizabad (*Encyclopedia Britannica*), from which King Dasaratha ruled his kingdom.

Bharat: Ancient name for the current Republic of India, Pakistan, Nepal, Bangladesh, and East Afghanistan.

Chithrakoota: Forest where Rama, Sitha, and Lakshmana first made a home when exiled.

Dharma: Ideal, righteous duty or moral behavior. In Hinduism, it is somebody's responsibility to behave according to strict moral and social codes; the religiousness earned by performing religious and social duties.

Five Elements: Earth, water, fire, air, and ether.

Karma: Fate.

Kiskindha: Kingdom ruled by Vali and later Sugreeva.

Kosala: Ancient kingdom of northern India, now known as Uttar Pradesh. Kosala extended across both banks of the Sarayu (modern Ghaghara) River and north into what is now Nepal. Kings descended from the sun ruled Kosala; one of these kings was King Dasaratha. (*Encyclopedia Britannica*)

Lanka: An island kingdom ruled by Rakshasas king, Ravana.

Mantra: Scriptural verses, incantations.

Mithila: Kingdom ruled by King Janaka.

Panchavati: Rama, Sitha, and Lakshmana's forest hut from which Sitha was abducted.

Payasam: A sweet preparation of milk and rice or sago.

Pooja: Religious worship.

Saastras: Sacred lore.

Tapas: Austerities and penances.

Vedas: Scripture: in four books.

Yaaga: Sacrifice.

Bibliography

Vaithiyanathan, Kurinchi Gnana. Tamil. *Kamba Ramayanam*. Unabridged. Prose. Prama Publishers, 2006.

Narayan, R. K. *The Ramayana.* Shortened Prose. Penguin Books, 1972.

Printed in the United States
By Bookmasters